THE ROAD T

MOTHERHOOD

WHERE THE JOURNEY BEGINS

JOANNE COOK

SUPPORTED BY

Copyright © 2025 Joanne Cook

ISBN 9798283817286 Paperback

First Published 2025 in Great Britain

The Publishing Pod 2025   www.thepublishingpod.co.uk

The Publishing Pod: Louisa Herridge & Jo Wildsmith

Cover Designer: Simon Clements

No part of this publication may be reproduced, stored in a retrieval system, or transmitted in any form or by any means, electronic, mechanical, by photocopying, recording, scanning, or otherwise, without the prior written permission of the author. No warranty may be created or extended by sales representatives or written sales materials.

This publication is designed to provide accurate and authoritative information in regard to the subject matter covered. It is sold with the understanding that neither the author nor the publisher is engaged in rendering medical, legal, financial, or other professional services. The author has used their best efforts in preparing this book, and the information herein is based on their own personal and professional experiences and findings.

The information provided in this book is intended for entertainment, general knowledge and educational purposes only and does not constitute medical advice. It is essential to consult with a qualified healthcare professional for any health concerns, diagnoses, or treatment recommendations.

The author and publisher disclaim any liability for any actions taken or not taken based on the information provided.

The author shall not be liable for any loss of profit or any other commercial damages, including but not limited to special, incidental, consequential, personal, or other damages.

All rights reserved.

This book is dedicated to:

My sons, Jack and Billy.

Having you both completed my world and I'm forever grateful I got to be your mum. Never let anything hold you back from achieving your dreams – this book is proof that dreams really do come true. Always live life on your terms and define your own happiness. You are both loved more than you will ever know and being your mum has been my proudest achievement by far.

Keep believing in yourselves because I will always believe in you both.

I love you both to the moon and back.

Contents

The Road to Motherhood: Where it Begins	1
Two Lines	5
Fruits of Labour	18
What They Forgot to Tell You	29
The Baby Name Battle	41
Hump, Bump and a Whole Load of Awkwardness	51
The Hormone Rollercoaster	58
The Final Push (Literally)	64
The Birth Story Lottery	70
Congratulations, It's Chaos!	77
The Mum Squad	85
The Road to Fatherhood	93
The Road to Fatherhood: Where it Begins	95
Two Lines	97
Fruits of Labour	101
What They Forgot to Tell You	103

The Baby Name Battle	107
Hump, Bump and a Whole Load of Awkwardness	109
The Hormone Rollercoaster	111
The Final Push (Literally)	113
The Birth Story Lottery	118
Congratulations, It's Chaos!	120
The Men Squad	123
Message from Jo	125
The Real Motherhood Diaries	131
About the Author	145

The Road to Motherhood: Where it Begins

There are twelve universal laws that govern the universe, but in motherhood, there is just one law that truly rules the world of mothers – Sod's Law.

Sod's Law is what may have led to you seeing two lines on a pee stick test, whether from a spontaneous night of passion, one too many drinks, or a planned pregnancy where your child was born on the day after the school intake year. Yes, Sod's Law is real and appears in every moment of 'The Road to Motherhood.'

When you found out you were pregnant in the middle of a career ladder promotion – Sod's Law was present.

The morning you had to be up early, but your baby decided to sleep in – Sod's Law was to blame.

A clean top that made you feel amazing, only to find yourself covered in baby vomit minutes later – Sod's Law was behind it all.

Sod's Law will appear in all corners of the world of mothers, along with society's expectations, comparison, emotions and changes in all areas of your life that no one ever prepared you for. Motherhood is the most rewarding and heartfelt role that you will ever encounter and the biggest experiment you will ever experience.

This is the first book in 'The Road to Motherhood' series and, as you embark on this journey, you will be wishing you had read these books before you first became a mum. In fact, you will be buying a copy for every pregnant and new mum you know because in reality there are no manuals or instruction booklets out there. Just stories from other mums and your own experiences which all have more bumps, roundabouts, and diversions than you had ever anticipated. This book series will take you back to reflect on each step of 'The Road to Motherhood,' the moments you forgot and the moments you felt like no one else understood.

There will be no nonsense inside this book about 'sucking it all up and getting on with it' – the kind of cover up that society expects you to do. No, everything will be kept real, relatable and unfiltered – the hilarious truths about becoming a mum that somehow you tried to forget, including questioning why your body has never been the same again.

Before you turn to chapter one, you are forewarned this book may come with side effects that may include lots of laughter, eye rolls and relatable chaos. The laughter moments will test your pelvic floor at times, and you will want to bite your tongue when you get to 'The Road to Fatherhood' version, which you can find at the end of this book.

Sit back, grab a cup of coffee (or a glass of wine if you have had one of those kinds of days) and let's take you back to where it all began with Book One about to begin.

Welcome to 'The Road to Motherhood.'

Two Lines

Let's be honest, there's no right time for a baby - except when you realise you're late!

AND THERE IT IS... that moment.

Wait... we have all heard the story of the birds and bees, so we don't need to go back to 'that' moment, even though right now it's making you smile thinking back to the night where your story began. Fast forward past the romantic evening, the drunken one-night stand or the quick occasion the kids were out of the house, whatever it was for you, we are fast forwarding to where it all really began. The moment where everything changed for you including your dignity! The next nine months, or potentially eighteen years of your life, all depended on the outcome of a pee stick test. The longest five-minute wait of your life.

Let me take you back to the toilet seat, not pleasant I know, but this is the place where it all began. For dignity purposes, we will call it the toilet stage, when you stepped up and recreated the

Niagara Falls scene. Before you waited for those lines to appear, you spent more time trying to work out the instructions on how to use the test stick – do you remember? I can imagine there were some harsh swear words involved in reading the simple instructions that did not make sense. The whole operation of opening the kit and peeing on a stick turned into an escape room challenge and a try-out for the Olympic precision peeing event.

As you sat on your toilet seat, you read:

Instructions to use test kit:

Step one: Open box and remove test stick from packaging.

Step two: Remove cap and place the test stick underneath urine at mid-flow and hold for five seconds.

Step three: Place the cap on the test stick and wait for five minutes. If two lines appear, pregnancy is confirmed. If one line appears, the test is negative. You can now dispose of the test in a suitable bin.

Now, how you actually interpreted these instructions:

Step one: Which end should I open? What part of the stick shall I hold? Will my fingers interfere with the test result if I touch the wrong end of the stick? Wait, let me find a video as these instructions are so unclear. OK got it. Remove cap. Where should I put the cap? Floor, no I can't have anything touching it as it might interfere with the results. OK I will place it on a piece of tissue on the floor. Right, ready for the next step.

Step two: This is easy, I can do this. Is it in the right place? Too late I'm peeing. Oh no it's not in the right place; I've peed on my hand! Yuk, this is disgusting, I can never tell anyone that this has happened. Quick move the stick, OK think it's in place now. How many seconds do I have to hold it under for? Was it four or five? Oh, I think I have missed the mid-flow. Damn too late. One, two, three, four, five... I'll give it a couple more seconds as I'm sure it needs more time, and they have written that wrong. I mean five seconds isn't long is it? Suppose I counted too fast? I'll give it more time, that way the result will be more accurate, OK six, seven, eight, nine, ten. Now what?

Step three: I need to replace the cap. I have just peed on my hand, will that matter? Oh gosh I need to hurry, the cap needs to go on, just put the cap on. Cap is now securely on, now to wait five minutes. I will set a timer on my phone. That is an idea, I could use the timer to cook a boiled egg next time, as I never seem to get it right. Back to the mission, why did eggs even come into my mind? Oh gosh is that a sign. I just need to wait. It won't take long. This feels long. This feels very long, shall I look? No, distract yourself. Find something to focus on. The test can't be positive; I am sure it is just a virus I have picked up. Yeah, I haven't been feeling 100% recently so no wonder I am late. Maybe I have mixed up my cycle dates and am not actually late after all. Oh, I can feel a stomach cramp, period is on its way so it can't be positive. How long do I have left? Thirty-four seconds. OK deep breath, nearly there and...

Two lines. Two positive lines. Two lines of certainty. Two lines and one word to follow.

This is the exact 'moment' I was referring to. Up until this point, many women like you and I have gone through the same process, all waiting to see what the next nine months have in store. Although many women share the same experience, seeing those two lines will have a different perspective, set of emotions and sense of reality for each woman. Each woman goes through this experience usually by themselves with only the toilet for support – and that is not referring to bottom support.

There are a thousand and one perspectives but let's take four different perspectives of women seeing those two lines. A response that you may well remember only too well.

If you were expecting this book to kick things off with the 'tears of joy' perspective, then this is a reminder that this book is not like most. Yes, the tears of joy perspective is experienced by many women as they are so excited to see those two lines, but in reality, that is not always the experience that every woman feels. Some of us will stare at those two lines with complete terror running through our emotions, followed by lots of swear words leaving our mouths. Thoughts of what on earth will happen next race through the mind – and fear of judgement from others will follow. A very different contrast to the planned experience of wanting and desiring to be pregnant. Some of us cry with joy and some of us cry with sheer panic.

Everything inside this book is being kept real and unfiltered. So, yes, I am starting with the, 'oh crap, how did this happen?' perspective. Do we really need any more books that paint society's perfect picture that every woman is excited and full of joy at seeing the two lines appear in front of her? Hell no, and I would not be honouring my own story of my first pregnancy if I did that. Starting with the happy, joyful tears reaction would be doing exactly what society does – putting a filter over motherhood. Society can shove their filters and us mums can support each other in owning every reaction women all around the world feel the moment we see our own two lines.

To the women who experienced the joyful moments, don't worry your perception is next. You will be glad in reading the 'oh crap' moment first and take a deep sigh that you remembered the science behind the birds and bees and sought out protection to never experience this kind of reaction until you were ready to be pregnant. From first-hand experience – it's one hell of a reaction when you really don't expect to see two lines!

Two Lines = 'Oh crap, how did that happen?'

You have probably bought this test because you're late and you're blaming some kind of virus or stress that is happening right now in your life, but let's be honest the birds and the bees created this somehow and truthfully you didn't listen to the sex education class at school. Remember the science behind the passion!

But yes, there are TWO Lines, two lines of assurance, 'It is positive.' Two lines of, 'Yes this is real,' and two lines of, 'What the hell am I going to do?'

This is the turning point, your body now suddenly feels different, and you probably are realising that you knew you were pregnant but didn't want to face up to it. There was a reason you started to pee on that stick, and it certainly wasn't just for fun and the price of a test could have bought you a bottle of wine!

Here come the emotions raging throughout your mind, there is nothing you can do as the emotions are in control right now. This was not planned and certainly not something you had thought would be a consequence of that 'one' night. Sorry chick, this is the part of the birds and the bees' story where you got stung by the bee! All you can do is breathe and continue to stare at those two lines until it feels real.

No, it's time to start screaming, crying or swearing – whatever comes out let it go girl! If only it was that easy to control all those emotions in that one moment and stay in control when you look at those two lines. Every reaction right now is valid, this wasn't part of a plan, it was not a surprise you were expecting, so own your right to these emotions.

Whether you are just about to step up the career ladder, planning to get married, don't want any more children or have just started a new relationship, the moment you see those two lines it will feel like your destiny has been taken out of your hands. Choices feel automatically confined and the judgement of other people's voices enter your head. This really wasn't good timing and right now your head is spinning with thoughts.

The 'oh crap how did that happen?' mummies-to-be at this point will work out who to call first. It will be like the game show where you get to call a friend for support. Which friend will listen, not give the judgemental or told you so conversation? This is really happening right now, and you just cannot believe it is happening to you.

Two Lines = 'We did it'

It can often be taken for granted that every woman will have children some day and somehow it will be easy to fall pregnant naturally. But in real life this isn't always the case, and my heart always goes out to people who try to fall pregnant and take these 'pee stick' tests so many times without seeing the double lines. It's amazing how the experience from seeing a single line can be everything to some but losing everything to another person.

The persistence, determination and everything that goes into trying for a baby to be disheartened by one single line is heartbreaking. However, when you finally see those two lines and your heart bursts with so much joy, tears flow because every part of you wants to scream that 'you did it' and in that moment no-one could take that warm feeling away from you. Two lines equals everything to you and so it should.

The universe has granted your wish. The two lines are just the beginning of your dream coming true. The 'we did it' kind of mummies-to-be at this point are the huggers of the world. They will reconfirm their joy with a hug from anyone around them – even strangers had better watch out as they will be on a mission to spread their joy!

This is the happiest day of their life right now.

Two Lines = 'Who's the daddy?'

Somehow this little 'pee stick' starts becoming a reality TV show and a 'who fathered this baby?' special.

In the moment of action, lust, passion and probably a drunken state, there was not one moment during that whirlwind action scene that you ever thought you would be sitting on a toilet waiting for the next nine months to be determined by the lines that are about to appear. Let's get real here, you were both in it for a bunk up, nothing more and nothing less. There were no plans whatsoever to become a baby machine for this guy – if there were, you would have probably drunk less alcohol that evening or stayed in alone with your pyjamas and a hot chocolate. But here you are, somehow you did and yes you also didn't listen in school to the 'birds and bees talk' either and now you have also got stung by the bee!

As you look down at the 'two lines' on your pee stick, you suddenly remember all the things you didn't like about this guy and start pointing out facial features that you hope your baby won't have because you had no interest in any relationship other than sex with him. You're young, free and single, so why would you care about a bunk up. It's easy to get caught up by the passion, but now you're here looking at the pee stick in disbelief at the two lines that have now tied you to this guy forever. You will be on the edge of the toilet seat in anticipation for what will feel like forever in hope to see just one line. But no there are two lines. The shock factor of emotions hit you and yes, you need that friend to talk to right now, as you can't even begin to digest the two little lines you have just seen.

Do you laugh, cry or scream? Everything you will do right now will be remembered as the shock factor moment of your life. You can already hear the silent sounds of judgement; the disapproving looks of 'you should have been more careful.' Right now, it is just you and the pee stick so telling anyone really can wait because you're having a baby, and you can't even have a glass of wine to digest the news! Yes, you're having a baby, and you need to be reminded time and time again until the shock wears off.

You guessed it, these mummies-to-be are not the huggable type from hereon. They have realised how much the 'personal' moments lead to unwanted surprises and begin to refrain from any human physical contact for the next 24, 48, 72 hours, and probably until they forget the birds and the bees story again later.

Two Lines = 'Well that was quick'

It's strange how for some it can take many months or years to become pregnant, yet for others it can happen so quickly. You can't quite believe the positive test. This moment is where the men begin to feel egotistically proud of themselves for having fast swimmers and yes, they will be smiling and sharing this proud moment with their friends.

You suddenly decided to have a baby and here it is, two little lines that confirm your plans. Two little lines that make you smile because right now you can't believe it happened that quickly. Now the doubting sets in and you begin to think maybe the test was faulty. The excitement, the rush, the full-on emotions of panic hit you. There is only one thing for you to do. Buy more tests!

So off you go on a *Supermarket Sweep* style shopping spree for a bundle of pregnancy tests. You will forget that each test costs you around ten pounds and just pile them into your basket. This is important. You need to validate the lines.

The lines are confirmed on each additional pee stick and a moment of happiness fills you. Although you now notice the cost of this validation is around hundred pounds, but you reassure yourself that it's OK as you needed to know. Right in this moment of endless confirmation of two lines, you start the planning stage all at once. Your diary exercises begin, working out how many weeks pregnant you are, when your maternity leave will start and you will start scheduling a date for your baby shower. You start to wonder who you will tell first or should you have a baby reveal? The rush of anticipated moments that bring you excitement and joy have only just begun. As you look in the mirror and rub your stomach you are sure you can see you're pregnant already – there definitely is a bump there!

Enjoy every moment of this because this is something you have desired, and your wish has come true. OK, maybe a little earlier than expected but for you that doesn't matter. You have got what you desired and now it's time for you to enjoy the next nine months of bliss (well hopefully bliss anyway).

Pregnancy planning mummies are the best at knowing all their monthly cycle dates. They will have everything ready to recall and work out. They become the event planners of the pregnancy world. The endless scan photos, the moments of reminding you they are pregnant and the smile that never leaves their face. They are the proud planner mummies of our world.

So, there you have it, four perspectives each with their own humour, moments of emotions – yet the same two lines. The start of The Road to Motherhood, that once appeared at you through a little test window, the start of everything you know today and still anticipating in the years ahead of you. The only thing in this world that can compare to the anticipation of waiting for those two lines to appear was the covid tests we were all using back in 2020. Two lines that hold so much power on your reaction, feelings and thoughts of what will be in store next.

There has always been one question I have had when it comes to pregnancy home testing kits. Why is it, with advanced technology, the same process of collecting the urine still applies? Have you noticed that the pee test stick results appear in different formats from two lines to displaying the words 'pregnant' or 'not pregnant,' but the exact same process of peeing onto a two-centimetre strip applies. Surely there is a more hygienic way to catch the mid flow than having to aim and fire without peeing on your own hand? There must be some kind of humour behind the scenes when designing these sticks. You can imagine a group of people all laughing at the size of the strip and hearing stories of how women are finding they have more pee on their hand than the stick. They must have a secret solution which has been developed alongside the technology but refuse to share, as the humour of these images brightens up their day. Why can't they provide a bigger container that collects the urine, and you dip the stick inside? Wait, don't the doctors test this way? Here unfolds the truth behind these home testing kits, they are designed to humour others – without them some of this chapter would have had less humour so for now we will keep them.

Entrepreneur mummies out there, this is your chance to expand your horizons and develop this idea, it may be too late for all of us as most of us have already been there and done that with trying to aim for the stick, but for other women new to this experience, there is still time. Let's revolutionise these pregnancy test kits and design a version that will help women to keep their dignity – well some of it anyway.

Before we move on to the next chapter, a little reminder. Always hug a pregnant woman in support of her emotions. Never shake her hand. Remember, she would have peed on her hand just before receiving the news and you won't be able to get that image out of your head once your hands meet.

Fruits of Labour

Your body is changing and no one prepared you for that, especially the grapes!

N O ONE PREPARED YOU for all the body changes that were going to happen during your pregnancy and after. Can you remember what your stomach looked like before? And ask yourself, has it ever felt the same since? From everything feeling perked during your pregnancy to everything just drooping the moment your first child came into the world. When women become mothers, they certainly learn that 'everything goes south,' very quickly. You will recall very easily the changes that pregnancy brought to your own body. Changes that others would not see at first sight, but you knew they were there. When you either saw them in the mirror reflection or from tightly squeezing your bum cheeks – you felt and saw the changes. It was the fruits of labour that began this whole transformative process that still leads you to question today the impact that having children really did have on your body, the bits they see and the bits they don't see.

Do you remember the pregnancy books that used to have a guide to inform you of the stages of the growing bump? The diluted version of the real facts that every woman would soon learn as she progressed into her pregnancy and realised it was not just a baby she was creating but also preparing a fruit salad. It is within these pregnancy self-help books that the reference to fruit began. At twelve-weeks the comparison of the growing fully formed baby to a little plum or passion fruit is a sweet reference and comforting by its small nature. But as you grow throughout the nine months of your pregnancy you are made to feel like a walking fruit salad bowl. Mangoes replace your apples as you progress month by month. The plum baby turns into an orange and then a watermelon. When people mention the birth, images of a baby's head are replaced by a picture of a watermelon passing through your vagina.

I am sure you could have written a more detailed overview of what actually was happening with your body – something like this:

'By now your whole body will feel like a fruit salad bowl. Your baby is growing nicely and fully formed like a little plum or passion fruit and your two apples will also begin to swell, making you look more perky than you ever have before. There is, however, another piece of fruit growing within you, not as you would expect. Welcome to the grapes. Yes, the bunch of forming grapes that hang just inside your bottom area that you will only notice on either going to the toilet or sitting down very sharply.

Apples to be proud of and grapes you would rather return for a refund. Be prepared – very prepared.'

The grapes come and go – sometimes still haunting you today, whether you still have them sprout out or just seeing them inside the supermarket bringing back memories. There really is no preparation for women to deal with the changes that the fruits of labour bring. The only people who will understand will be the Mum Squad.

As Mum Squad members, it is only fair for us women to prepare future generations of pregnant women to inform them of what is to come within the fruits of labour. So here it is, the guide that will accompany the visuals from the fruit aisle within the supermarket.

The Grapes – The Piles Nightmare

Yes, let's start with the grapes whilst we are onto the topic of them. The tiny little bundle of PILES – a word society doesn't speak out loud. Yes, the unspoken word of PILES. There is no proud ownership in talking about them. The embarrassment of having piles, the quiet talk of them to make sure they go undiscovered to the listening ears of the many. If you have never referenced them as grapes, now is a chance to get your phone out and compare them. The word grapes being less embarrassing to reference them to. The little bunch of piles hits most women in their pregnancy journey – before and after, they were there waiting for you, ready to pounce and pop up still from time to time.

So why are they called piles? This definition may help:

P – Pressure: That moment you realise these 'grapes' are not for a fruit salad but for sitting uncomfortably for weeks.

I – Inevitable: Because, apparently, no pregnancy journey is complete without them.

L – Leaning: As in, you will become a pro at leaning on one cheek to avoid grape-crushing agony.

E – Exaggeration: When your partner says, 'It can't be that bad,' and you give them that look of, 'I will shove something where the sun doesn't shine,' to see how they would feel.

S – Surprise: Because no one warned you that pregnancy could turn your bottom into a vineyard that feels like it is set on fire.

They come out of nowhere, they sneak up behind you and then they ATTACK – full blown can't sit down ATTACK! Yes, I recall this experience and what's more I even recall the conversation my husband had with his boss on suitable remedies to help me – and yes, a very detailed conversation that was. The cheek of it, looking back and still feeling the frustration of them discussing my private little bundle. They were my private little friends, yes, suddenly I found myself becoming very protective about my little grapes as they were being spoken of in a workplace full of men. How dare they try to fix them, they are a part of me, not them? Yes, they are uncomfortable, but they are private and not up for discussion, after all we don't talk about piles in public – do we?

Although their advice was not welcomed, they did have many remedies, which as you may imagine consisted of using a rubber ring. I am still trying to figure out if this advice was from them watching their own wives go through the drama of piles or them themselves – somehow the thought of these men all sitting on rubber rings is lightening the situation right now. But yes, rubber rings are the antidote to piles and the saviour of many butts.

For pregnant women and new mummies, the rubber ring becomes your next best friend – honestly! You will recall how you convinced yourself that sitting on a rubber ring is quite normal. There was one problem with using a rubber ring for those of you who already had young children. Imagine sitting there comfortably and then your three-year-old comes into the room and says very loudly, 'Why is mummy sitting on my swimming ring?' tugging it away from you. You sit firmer and stare directly at your child because right in that moment it is a will of power and no matter who wins the rubber ring it will have consequences on the hanging grapes. Here is the problem... in that moment, you have two choices. Choice A: stand up and fight for your beloved saviour of a rubber ring – are you ready to let go? Or Choice B: give in and sit back on that uncomfortable chair and watch your child put their swimming aid away – glaring at them with the thought that you will find it once they go to bed that evening.

Either way, you have some explaining to do to a three-year-old who, let's face it, will not have a clue what you're talking about if you explain you need it for your piles and probably tell everyone at school, 'Mummy has got grapes shoved up her butt and stole my swimming ring.' I will leave you to recall your own explanation, but either way your grapes are public knowledge from this point – kids are not afraid to openly talk about piles.

Having children does not free you from any grape bundle, in fact it is the one thing that is guaranteed to pop up when you least expect them. Piles do not discriminate, and Sod's Law loves to engage in their presence.

The Apples – The Great Boob Expansion

Do you ever look back on your pregnancy and wish you still had those perked apples that gave a model from Victoria Secret a run for her money. Ahh, the boob job that just happened overnight without any invasive prodding. The delight of having to go up a bigger cup size and everywhere you walked the boobs led and you followed. Now, you're looking down and wondering what the hell happened. As quickly as they arrived, the quicker they left – transforming into two hanging fruits that had no resemblance to the ones you had even before you had kids.

There is one memory of the perky apples you are glad that is in the past and that is the itching. The moments you would scratch like a toddler with chicken pox, knowing you shouldn't but you couldn't resist. As the boobs grew bigger each day, the itching got out of control. Google would really have been your best friend at this moment. You couldn't help yourself to give the odd scratch in public or run to the toilet to give them one hell of a scratch because they became the most annoying part of your body – especially in the hot weather.

Not all moments of admiration are watching your apples grow. In fact, the bigger they grew, the more you wanted to rip off the bra and set the girls free – and not for any spiritual feel free moment but because it gets so damn hot in there. Pregnancy boobs are the heat traps that you had never felt before. There is a joyous feeling, that only women understand, and that is the feeling when you take off your bra – the feeling that no matter what stage you are in your life still feels good. A feeling that makes you want to break out into the song lyrics from, 'What a Feeling.'

The Peach Glow

The societal myth that all women expect to receive in pregnancy is the hope that when you wake up after receiving two lines on a pregnancy test that your skin will suddenly bloom into a peachy glow that others are in envy of. In reality, the peach refers more to the puffy features and feet that would present themselves on hot days and the skin tone is more red than peach as you became hot and flustered.

All those baby books back then forgot to mention the revisitation of your pubescent spots. The sudden little creatures that appear overnight. Instead of breaking out into radiance it was more like the breakout itself of puberty hitting you once again.

The puffy peach feel ran through your body from the head right down to your feet. Yes, the peachy puffiness of swollen ankles reminding you that you are filled with more water than ever.

The Watermelon

One day you were admiring this little bump growing, turning from a tiny plum into an orange and then suddenly it became a watermelon. No more admiration at the growth other than a reminder that it had to pass through your vagina soon and that you could no longer walk in a straight line.

The watermelon left you waddling like a duck and taking over most of the bed because there really was no comfortable position to sleep in. As you tried to reach, let alone try to see your toes, the watermelon prevented it all. Putting on socks was more like going on a mission to Mars, preparing a toe to hook one part of the sock and then a mighty pull in hope that it was on in seconds because the mission alone exhausted you.

Then there was the floor test. The constant test throughout the pregnancy to determine the day when you simply could pick up something from the floor without wobbling over and feeling like an eighties weeble toy.

And finally, the watermelon movements. As your baby moved you would have had your own reactions to this. For some it can be the reassuring movement they longed to feel and for others it will feel like a scene out of the film Alien. Some of you, like me, may have had a stubborn watermelon that decided it was not going to play ball and move around, instead leaving you counting the movements on a tick sheet and leaving the last minimal kick to the last second just as you're about to hit the hospital. The stubborn babies who showed you who really was in control. The same applied whenever you wanted someone else to feel the movement and they decided now wasn't the time to play. Yes, most of us have that one child who did this, and we are now looking at them and now connecting the dots to where their stubborn personality came from.

The Watermelon Rind Effect

Yes, we are still on watermelons, as whilst one grew inside of you the skin was appearing around you – and fast! Your first introduction to the watermelon rind aka stretch marks would have not been a pleasant one, even for those of you who did all they could to prevent them. The moment you see a stretch mark streak across your stomach, thighs or boobs you would have felt like a tiger earning her stripes. For part of you appreciates these as the tattoos of motherhood and the other part of you would have been trying to work out a way to get rid of them fast.

Stretch marks are both unpleasant yet powerful markings that most mothers choose to hide but also, they are a reminder of the difficult times that had to be endured. Now, this evening you will no doubt be looking at your own stomach area to see if you can still see them.

There is one thing about your stretch marks that is more annoying than seeing them appear and that is someone counting them. Whether it was your partner or junior doctor, it was an unpleasant experience to hear and could have resulted to you unleashing your hormone sister Raging Rita, taking no responsibility for squeezing their plums in response to the delight on their face at discovering them.

The Lemon Squeeze

Pregnancy sickness is not just the feeling of wanting to throw up every second – it feels like sucking on a sour, bitter lemon with a taste that never leaves you. For some it is a matter of weeks and for others, you will be shouting, 'Weeks more like the whole nine months!' Yes, sickness grips every woman in a different way, some luckily escape it, and some spend their nine months back in the toilet.

There is one thing about sickness that most of you will recall and that is the blaming of specific foods and drinks that caused it. You dare not blame your child standing there in front of you, how could you? This sweet innocent child that you brought into the world. No, it would have been the curry sauce from the last takeout, the apple juice that turned sour or the smell of something that passed you by. Yes, some of this didn't help but the truth is your bundle of a watermelon was causing this, and you really do have them to thank.

The Banana

It all started with the banana. Yes, we all know about the banana's role in the fruits of labour, so let's keep the picture painted in our own minds. Bananas have a lot to answer for and were the reason your body felt like a fruit salad back then – that is all I am saying on this fruit.

So, there you have it, your body was once stretched, pulled, puffed out and resembled a fruit salad that society expects you to bounce back from – spoiler for those of you still waiting – it doesn't. Motherhood creates a new version of your temple, one that bears the stripes of bravery, the jelly belly that still wobbles from carrying a watermelon and objects pointing down south. Yet it was the most marvellous thing you could have ever achieved in your life, another human created inside of you. For some of you, it's just the beginning and you have more little humans to create – good luck because you know what fruit awaits you after the banana!

What They Forgot to Tell You

One life, two very different realities that somehow forgot to be shared with you!

THERE IS ONE THING, one very important thing, that no-one ever prepared you for when you were pregnant. Something others, even other mums, didn't mention, apart from a few odd sarcastic remarks or jokes that left you questioning what they meant. Not the birth stories, which everyone feels the need to share, not the sleepless nights, no, we are talking about YOU – who you *were* versus who you *became* the moment you found out you were pregnant.

Think about Clark Kent vs Superman, the unpolished vs polished identities of one person. For you that is You vs Mum-You. These are two complete identities that feel like they have their own separate lives and is something that you wished you had prepared yourself for before your children came into the world because when that question hits you – it hits you bloody hard. 'Who am I?'

'The Road to Motherhood' is not just a journey from conception to motherhood, it's a complete transformation of who you were to who you became. It's within these newfound identities that are not created over time but seamlessly an overnight transformation that you had no part in – only as the observer when you look into the mirror and ask yourself, 'What happened to the polished version of me?'

Deep within the creation of these identities there will be many unpolished versions of you that you wouldn't even recognise. You catch yourself saying something out loud that goes in the opposite direction of a thought you once had. You do things that you never thought you would do before, and you experience situations that really make you feel on the opposite end of the woman you once were. But it is only now you recall these traits, back then you may have not even noticed them. Were any of these traits yours?

Who am I?

Let me introduce you to some characters... do you recognise any of these traits in the search to recognise who you are now?

Love at First Sight Lucy

The trait of seeing beauty in everything of your child. This usually begins the moment you are laying on a bed waiting for the image to appear on the screen at your first scan appointment. As you wait in anticipation, with an anxious wait to check everything is OK, you hold your breath and there it is. An image you fell instantly in love with. Your baby. You may have uttered the words, 'They are so cute!' As you stare at the screen, all you can see is beauty and love – others would disagree, not because your baby isn't beautiful or indeed cute, but because the image you're referring to looks more like a potato baby.

For anyone else, the image represents a potato shape with no resemblance to the child you have today. You became in love at first sight with your baby and forever will recall how cute they are from social media announcements, pictures and showing off moments. Your baby, or now child, is the cutest of them all. However, there was a time when you would have frowned upon this comment. A time when someone would have said, 'Isn't my baby cute?' and you would have seen a completely different cuteness, perhaps a resemblance to a 1980s cabbage patch doll – two completely different perspectives. You would also now frown at a person if they even tried to resemble your child to these dolls. But here you are now fully transformed with the love at first trait that will stay with you forever.

Checklist Charlotte

The moment you see the scan image you get instant reassurance that everything is OK, this reassurance has been long awaited since you saw those two lines. When every person said everything would be OK, you didn't believe them until you saw your little potato yourself. The problem is this reassurance lasted all but 24 hours, in fact the moment you got into the car park you were wondering how long it would be until your next appointment. Gone were the days you were free from worry and would go with the flow, people once knew you as In-the-Moment Charlotte and now you have resulted in becoming Checklist Charlotte with a list of questions to ask the midwife next time.

It wasn't just the baby's health you sought reassurance for, no, it was for all areas of your pregnancy. From eating something and wondering if what you just swallowed was on the banned food list for pregnant mums and then purchasing every baby product 'just in case' you needed it – now you had become queen of checklists and mistress of worry.

Back then you would have had hauled supplies of nappies, milk, and wipes (and many other things) all stockpiled as if we were heading into lockdown. You had to be prepared, reassured, and tried to overcome the worry by purchasing another 'must needed' item. You had enough baby supplies to kit out a whole maternity unit, but reassurance was the key here and nothing else mattered.

Fact Checking Fiona

You were once known for not having a care in the world when it came to eating, drinking, engaging experiences and were known for your dare devil moments. But the moment you saw your little baby image on the screen something changed and suddenly you needed to know every fact before engaging in anything. Pregnancy for you was a serious operation and one that was taken seriously in every moment.

From checking the foods you could and couldn't eat to making sure everyone around you had the list when you were invited out for dinner. Before you attempted to travel you would check with the GP, only to be told you do not need permission to travel one hour in a car to your in-laws' house – that may have been you trying to get out of visiting them but either way you sought the permission. You checked the weather for appropriate clothing for your bump, reframed from any physical contact from your partner until you received confirmation that his presence would not squash the baby. You had every app and Google at the ready to make sure you were prepared for any fact searching activity – that was the closest to in-the-moment you became again.

Spectacular Sarah

Birthdays, anniversaries, celebrations – yes you once celebrated but much preferred a close encounter with a small group of family and friends. That was until you too saw your little bundle of joy on the screen where you turned into a spectacular event planner. Yes, the sudden urge to go all out celebrating with an extravagant gender reveal and a party for everyone. There was the coloured themed reveal cake, the balloon, the confetti cannon and even the white doves that carried a coloured ribbon. You would have hired an airplane with a banner if your partner had not put the stop to the madness. Yes, not one way to reveal but several. Your guests would be showered in delights and no expense spared. A grand entrance, special makeshift stage to let everyone know the gender of your baby. The only thing that would ever spoil this is if your baby decided to be stubborn at the scan and kept their legs crossed. You waited in anticipation, booking more than one scan as the thought of this happening and spoiling your spectacular show of a gender reveal. What guests didn't realise was that you had the next event already lined up – the baby shower and the whole event planning began the day after the reveal party – only this time even bigger!

Freedom Fanny and Denial Danielle

The contrast between these two is immediately obvious when they sit down for a conversation. If you were a Freedom Fanny, you would have been worried already that this little image on the screen was going to change your life forever. Yes, we are talking about freedom here with Fanny, nothing else, so please refocus your mind. Freedom Fanny would hold her head in her hands asking her partner, friend or family member if she really could do this. The shock, the reality that she may not have the freedom she once knew. Denial Danielle, however, would reassure her that no baby was going to change her life. She would do things differently and doesn't understand how all these mums can tell her that a baby will change her life. Her view was very much that she was in control, and it would only change her life if she let it. Unlike Freedom Fanny with her head in her hands, Denial Danielle, simply stood with shoulders tall, head held high, and lips closed. She was not going to be like any other mum – she had it all planned out – well, so she thought.

Babyzilla Beth

The once quiet, go with the flow woman who sat in the background of any conversations, events or meetings had now turned into a complete transformation like the hulk. From the moment she laid eyes on her little potato she became the worst pregnant woman of all – a Babyzilla. Yes, nothing was right, and everyone was ordered into line. There were schedules, job descriptions, codes of conduct for the delivery room and lists galore. Babyzilla Beth has turned into something that no one could quiet understand what had happened to her – all they dreaded was the birthing room where most people were lucky to escape, except her birthing partner who had to read the birthing plan every day right up to the delivery so that they got each request right.

The Babyzilla Beths remind everyone they are pregnant and refuse to do anything they feel is not within the parameters of a pregnant woman. They will push out their stomachs in hope to get a seat and they will have total control of colour coordinating the nursery, baby clothes and coming home procedures. Fortunately, they do calm down and revert to their quiet self after birth unless they plan a wedding after and just may become a bridezilla.

Calendar Clare

The most disorganised of all women you will find, who once would forget birthdays, events and anything in her personal diary. Most would recall Calendar Clares as women who need to be reminded of everything – including her own menstrual cycle!

However, the moment she sees her little spud on the screen, everything changes. She suddenly has her calendar highlighted with each appointment, colour coordinating which appointment is for the doctor, and which is for the midwife. She buys folders to store her appointment letters and reads through her maternity notes with a fine-toothed comb to make sure she doesn't miss anything. Suddenly, here comes a woman who is setting reminders, working out specific dates and being congratulated for her organisation skills. Little do they realise this change of habit is simply down to maximising as much time away from work as possible. Yes, the planning of long weekends, half days and extended leave on the back of an appointment. Calendar Clares know exactly how to make the dates work in their favour!

Memory Lane Molly

The woman who once would spring clean her flat every month and throw away anything that hadn't been used in the last six weeks. The overnight changes started with a vision of her little baby image too, but may have occurred from the moment she saw two lines on her pregnancy test. Yes, you guessed it she kept her pee stick. The woman who was not ashamed of peeing on her stick and putting it into a memory box to reflect on in years to come. From this point on, Memory Lane Molly would collect anything from scan images, leaflets, cards, photos of her and the hospital staff, monthly mirror pictures of her growing watermelon and anything that resembled the journey she had undertaken on 'The Road to Motherhood.' The Memory Lane Mollys don't usually lose their trait after birth and are the ones who tend to have the cards with the baby confirming how old they are month by month. The umbilical-cord clip, their first sock, baby-grow and not just one – everything. She piles the top of her wardrobes with clothes that no longer fit her growing baby in hope one day another child will wear them, but, in all honesty, she can't part with the memories of the day her baby looked cute in that outfit – cute in one hundred outfits.

Maternity Matilda

The countdown to maternity leave queen is actually the woman who used to find it hard to take a break or go on annual leave as the office may need her. Gone were the days where her boss had to force her to book in the annual leave and now, she has become the queen of planning the dates of her exact maternity leave departure. Maternity Matilda had an agenda to not only count down but to inform everyone within the office that she would be leaving to have a baby. Not once or twice, but an email sequence just in case they forgot the first one. Subtle reminders of craving biscuits in the kitchen and rubs of the tummy in meetings, there was no way she could go on leave without the office send off – and she wasn't leaving that to chance. So out came the countdown calendars clearly seen by all on her desk, marking each day off with a red cross. When others asked how long she had left, she knew the exact months, weeks, days, hours and probably minutes. There was one thing that someone forgot to share with Maternity Matilda and that was her vision for maternity leave which was a picture she had painted of daytime TV, walking in the sunshine, visiting family, friends, and mother groups. Yes, the smile upon her face every time she mentioned her leave would meet with another mum who had returned and wanted to tell her exactly what was in store – but didn't want to burst the bubble. Yes, from stirrups in the birthing room, to late night heartburn which prevented any daytime TV watching as she would simply be too exhausted to get out of bed. Trips to family and friends whilst pregnant would be limited to her not being able to fit behind the wheel and mother groups would become a mission to even plan out. Yes, Maternity Matilda's stayed in her bubble until the first week of her leave, when reality hit.

No matter what, there is that huge dilemma of when to start maternity leave. This all important 'get out of jail' kind of card of extended leave had to be planned well. The problem here is Sod's Law and its role in the all-important date. Would she plan to go for two weeks before the due date to be met with an early arrival? Would she work up until her due date to find herself not being able to move to get into the office? Or perhaps her baby would decide on staying put for another two weeks which would result in a wasted month of maternity leave. Whatever date she planned, Sod's Law would be there ready to shake things up, but no one dared tell Maternity Matilda that!

These are some of the adopted personality traits you may be familiar with or glad they didn't form part of your hormone cycle in your pregnancy. Either way, you will have experienced a transition from the woman you once were to who you have now become. One life and two very different realities to what was in store – but you know that already because you are living that right now. So, grab the coffee and reheat it for the third time – you will get a chance to drink it finally and get ready to move onto the next chapter. You may need a biscuit too for this one!

The Baby Name Battle

Trying to pick baby names is just a process of eliminating everyone you've ever disliked and making sure the name doesn't rhyme with fanny.

H AVE YOU EVER THOUGHT about your own name and how life could have turned out quite differently if your parents had messed this up completely? I mean, your whole life outcome was once in the hands of your mum especially, who may have been going through the worst body changes of all time and blaming the little sprog, aka you. Imagine if she had thought, 'I will teach you a lesson,' and called you something completely inappropriate just to have the last laugh. If you are planning more children, note that this really should not be done and please think of your child as the name will forever be called across the school playground. The choosing of a name comes with huge responsibility. If you think about friends you were with at school, colleagues, and names you have heard perhaps on the television, you can see which adults were taking the job of naming their child seriously.

So, there you were with a little plum growing inside of you, recalling the names you once called your baby doll as a child in hope one day you could call a real baby that name. Sweet, cute little names that have followed you through to the moment where all your dreams would be answered until you hear the words from your partner, 'I don't like that name.' Seriously, years of holding this name, securing the name from all your friends and family over the years to be told he didn't like the name. Now, depending on you as a person and your pregnancy at the time you may have been easy-going and just feel disappointed or you may have secretly called your baby this name whilst rubbing your tummy thinking that you will get your own way in the end. Either way, this name that holds value for decades is the chosen one until...

The Name Grabbers Stole It

You found out your friend or a family member had just called their baby this name. Yes, the utter cheek of these people calling their baby your baby's name. The betrayal of getting in first and sealing the deal on the birth certificate, how dare they? The name didn't even suit their baby, and it was your baby's name! At this point, you stumbled in a hormonal crying fit, vowing to never ever disclose a name again and refusing to call the child by the name that belongs to your growing plum. Things could turn nasty right now but no, you picked yourself up and your plum... and possibly grapes depending on if the vine has made an appearance, and you shrugged it off with a carefree attitude and a determination to find a better name.

Looking back, the moment you secure your child's name you should have had it trademarked, no bugger could have used it then, although you can forget how many other kids hold the same name. The audacity of people stealing your name right in front of you left you questioning their overall motives of authenticity towards you because IT WAS YOUR NAME NOT FOR THEM TO TAKE. Another fit of crying continued again as you really couldn't get over it.

There Was a Kid with That Name in the Class You Were Teaching or Your Child Attends

This is the hardest because the moment you recognise a child who you really didn't take a liking to have the same name as your unborn baby – disaster happens. There is no time for tears, but a brainstorming event scheduled to find another name because there is no way you are calling your child that name because the image of the other child will pop into your head every time and you can't have that. So, off you went to research the baby name books, writing name choices down all whilst your partner thought you were simply just crazy as in their view it doesn't matter if they had the same name. There is something about a name that brings instant recall of another child or adult that you dislike and, no matter what, there is no way you will continue with your name choice. Baby doll or not, it has to go!

Jack and Jill Went Up the Hill

Yes, the rhyming problem. The name you liked but figured out (usually from someone else) that it rhymes with something else that is unmentionable or together with your surname is a complete no. What did you do? You spent hours trying to work out if it really did matter and would it matter as your baby grows because over time surely people will act more maturely and not rhyme it with anything. The giggles around you become louder and you realise that this would never be forgotten. Your partner constantly mentions it and reminds you that you can't do that to your poor little child. The disappointment sets in and you're back to the drawing board, only this time sarcastically running each name through everyone's point of view.

Name choices can seriously go wrong, and you may have known that person with a surname like 'Condom' and laughed. Yes, somewhere you would have heard the surname being called, but imagine the power of the parents naming their child Richard because they simply always wanted that name for a boy. The shortening for Richard is 'Dick' so if you add the surname, you have completely set your child up for the future school playground being known as Dick Condom. You can imagine sitting in a hospital waiting room as an adult and being called by the nurse 'do we have a Dick Condom here?'

Seriously it can go so wrong with just a name you like and really hadn't thought about the logistics.

Here are other disasters that could have potentially ruined your own children's name path (or yours!):

Jack Danny – Fanny

Richard Head – Dick Head

Ben Dover – Bend Over

Anna Conda – Anaconda

Helen Back – Been to hell and back

Anita Bath – I-need-a-bath

The point is right then when you were naming your child it probably never even crossed your mind that names could be the biggest problem you will have. There is always someone that will reframe it into a rhyme, a song lyric or an advert like above. So really the name choices are up to you but a word of warning, if you are going to consider naming your child after a piece of fruit such as apple or pear, just remember you may still be connecting to the maternal fruits of labour spoken of in a previous chapter. Names should also be thought of wisely as a whole person's life outlook could all have a different path if the wrong name has been chosen.

It should also be worth noting that people who name their babies after the place they conceived should really think clearly about their holiday and hotel locations beforehand, as again this can end totally crazily, especially in a cost-of-living crisis where budget locations don't usually have the same name feel as a luxury one. There is a big difference between hotel Costa-De-Spam and hotel Ocean Princess Pearl. The name will forever determine your relationship with your teenager – so please think wisely or have enough money saved to get a deed poll name change for when they are older if they wish.

Just for the record, you can't be accountable for phrases and names used once you have already chosen your child's name. Can you imagine the poor women called Karen and Nelly who consistently get referred to as 'don't be a Karen' or a 'negative Nelly.' The poor Karens and Nellys of this world who do nothing but get on with their day-to-day lives and yet get pulled into email complaints regardless of the person's name they are forever known as 'Karen or Nelly.' Sorry Karens and Nellys reading this book, I will apologise on behalf of society to you. I have no idea how this came about other than there must have been one hell of a complaint letter written and signed off by a real person called 'Karen' where the name then became trademarked in society as the complainer of all complainers. This must be also true for the Nellys out there. It started off with one woman called Nelly who was honestly having the worst time in life and was lacking the positive gene whilst surrounding herself with her girlfriends, resulting in her too trademarking the name Nelly in society as the negative one. Please don't be Karen or Nelly and enter my inbox about this reference, I truly believe we should overcome the society trademarks and not have your name brought into the negative pathways of complaints and downtimes in life. I thank you women for not sending me any negative correspondence to my inbox to prove me wrong, especially as I write this with love and am here to stand tall with the Karens and Nellys of the world. I also apologise for any partners out there called Dick and people referring to 'don't be a Dick.' I mean, what is wrong with Dicks – or is that just opening up a completely separate conversation?

Whatever name you chose, you would have done so from a place of desire and love so don't worry if right now you are trying to find every rhyme for each of your children before your child does. It may be worth checking any names your partner picked to ensure they didn't come from a football team player, celebrity or actor/actress from their favourite film – children hate this kind of stuff especially if the kids at school find out. Forever hold on to your child's birth certificate in remembrance of the responsibility you once had and if your child is ever on a self-discovery journey trying to think what on earth were you thinking when you named them, I would blame your partner as there is no going back when the name battle commences!

You may also want to check out the initials of names because this also counts in the name battle, apparently. I have a great information source from the male population that yes, initials do count, so I hope you made wise choices back then too. Naming your child Ben Jameson may sound OK but in society having 'BJ' as initials references to something that they do not want to be known as. Honestly the name battle will be one of the hardest decisions of all time, it will make the birthing plan look like a piece of cake.

Then we have the traditionalists – was that you? Naming your child after their dad to keep the name in the family, where you end up having so many James Juniors to the name you then begin to call them Big James, Small James, Suzie's James, Cousin Once Removed James. Literally a family all with the same name and somehow it seems to work that everyone knows who you are talking about. Thankfully with big families it is not often everyone gets together in one room for Christmas because Secret Santa would certainly lead to confusion.

It doesn't end there because then we have the traditional names spelt differently to add a personal spin on it. Usually, it starts with a simple change from a 'y' to an 'ie' then we add the hyphens and the silent letters followed by an 's' being replaced by a 'z' and so on. It is one hell of a confusing situation when writing out these names – ask any schoolteacher, I am sure they would agree. Yes, it is great to be unique, but it can lead to your child having to consistently say, 'That is not how you spell my name.'

When we gave our children a name what we were really doing was giving them an identity without even realising it. An identity that the name holds from previous shoes it has walked in whilst others observed. We have the names that are labelled 'naughty children,' 'loud children,' 'misbehaved children,' 'cheeky children,' – you get where I am going with this. One name can completely transform your child's identity. The funniest thing is that there will actually be coincidences in these names being grouped. You will try to challenge it by saying your little Thomas is no way a naughty child and suddenly, as you defend his honour, he has just painted your washing machine and stuck his tongue at you when you scream, 'No don't do that.'

Names don't just have an identity, they apparently have a look about them. Jacks apparently look like Jacks, Sarahs looks like Sarahs, and so on. How many parents decide on a name at birth to completely change it when they see their little bundle because they didn't look like the name they had chosen? Look at how many people will say your child looks like their name – what does this even mean? How can a baby being formed in their mother's stomach grow without a name but then suddenly look like a name that wasn't given until birth. Have we all just gone mad, or do we listen to so much crap that we believe it – and say it? Yes, we have all done it somehow.

The name battle doesn't end when your child is born, it continues throughout because they will always wish you had called them something else and forever hold it against you should you have chosen a name they don't like or is too old fashioned. This isn't just teenagers we are talking about, no, five-year-olds will try to change their name too but usually because they want to be called Spiderman or randomly picking John. From common names, unique names and names that you can't even pronounce, there is a name battle for them all.

There is one thing that is for certain when it comes to names and that is everyone will always know a Dave.

Hump, Bump and a Whole Load of Awkwardness

There's nothing that kills the mood more than the thought two little eyes can see you.

NO ONE EVER MENTIONED to you the complicated logistical nightmare of how to get it on with a bump when you were pregnant. It's funny that there were many women around telling you the best way to sleep, eat and deal with the annoying heartburn but when it came to the bedroom department the closest you got to advice was someone telling you to shove a pillow between your legs to balance you out whilst sleeping. Your entire sex life whilst pregnant didn't just become an experiment but a full-on physical workout – and that was you just trying to position yourself.

Between back aches, sore boobs, swollen ankles and a bladder that just never felt empty, it is a surprise any of us even wanted to attempt it. There is nothing to make you feel sexier than the constant reminder of the bump in front of you and the call out of 'I need another pillow.' The whole act becomes an Olympic show with a whole load of awkwardness. The pre-intimate conversations of mapping out the logistics and talking about the fears, to the juggling act and then the afterthoughts – gone are the days you could get caught up in the passion and forget what was going on around you. If it wasn't the awkwardness of the physical complexities and conversations, the biggest turn off was the thought of those two little eyes watching the whole act, which felt so wrong. The moment that thought landed into your minds it was game over. When they say babies are the biggest contraceptives – they were not wrong.

By the time you enter the last phase of pregnancy, your sex life becomes a game of Twister meets Jenga. One wrong move and everything collapses – including your dignity.

If you think your sex life has its complications now that you've got kids, cast your mind back to when you were pregnant – because believe me it was way more complicated back then. You can list the passion killers as many times as you like from sleepless nights to toddler tantrums, but these are nothing compared to the logistical nightmare of trying to get it on with a baby bump that looked like a space hopper. Seriously, how on earth did anyone ever think pregnancy and sex could include romance.

Yes, you may even recall that sex and pregnancy was a no-go zone for you, and you are now thankful that you didn't go there as you can't imagine having to work through the logistics. Here are some you may or may not have experienced:

The Awkward Logistics You Had to Consider

Finding the Right Angle – That night of passion may have felt like a Rubix cube with lots of twists and movements to find that friendly bump position.

The Cushion Dilemma – Pillows and cushions took on a new role and not for romance. Inserting cushions into gaps for support felt like a game of Tetris. The nights of passion needed a good plan beforehand, that was for sure.

Belly Bumper Cars – There was a lot of bumper car action as the belly would get in the way at times – accidental of course and a constant reminder there is a baby inside.

The Baby Watching Fears

Can the baby see us? Suddenly your night of passion was filled with thoughts of 'can the baby actually see you both?' and the biggest contraceptive of all times.

What if It Shakes the Baby? The thought of your baby now being placed on their first bouncy castle will be another reason for a natural end to the start of what the raging hormones thought would end in a good night. No, baby won't shake but the thought did shake both your minds to stop at the time.

Your Partner's Perspective

Does the size matter? Yes, your partner felt that their pride and joy was too sizeable for the act of passion as they believed they have a measurable size that would poke the baby. No matter how much reassurance you gave, it was either a conversation you went with and let them believe this size of ego or a conversation that dented the ego of their manhood – a touchy conversation either way. No, it won't touch the baby's head.

How gentle and caring should I be? The night of passion combined with the fear your significant other has for your care and attention could lead to you being petted like a puppy mid-way to offer you reassurance.

The Sudden Cramp Attack

When your leg decides to have a muscle cramp right in the middle of action and after finding a comfortable position. The spasm that kills the romance and the awkward moment your partner stops in action to rub your leg whilst trying to reassure you to stay in the mood. Faces go from passion to panic in seconds.

The Unfortunate Sound Effects

Gone were the days of 'oohs and aahs' which were replaced by the body making unwanted sound effects of its own at any moment in the operation of passion. The unexpected fart that happens right in the middle and you both just freeze and burst out giggling whilst you quickly cover up that the baby must have been laying on your colon somehow. The oohs are replaced with ouches as you forget in the moment that you can't flip over in seconds and the ahhs replaced with 'Are we done yet?' moments when you truly have had enough of playing Tetris.

With your first it was hard and your second it was even harder. Yes, by the second pregnancy you would have experienced all the above plus the juggling skills of finding the right time when your other child was asleep whilst also trying to keep your ears open. Let's face it, sex from pregnancy onwards is never the same spontaneous act and you can see why so many make up the excuse of having a headache because in reality the logistics is the biggest passion killer of all.

Just when you thought the logistical nightmare of having sex whilst pregnant was over, the post-baby intimacy hurdle comes next. There is nothing more worrying than wondering if all your bits have healed and been put back into place. Counting the weeks of recovery and wondering what the transformation of motherhood has done to your vagina post pregnancy. No longer fears around the bump and more around the vagina walls, leaving you wondering if the pelvic floor exercises would have come in useful right now. You would think surviving sex whilst pregnant would make you a pro but no, there is a whole other level of awkwardness when it comes down to the deed. You may have survived the labour, stitches or a reconstruction but the thought of anything prodding you down there will give anyone a headache. As you know though, you have to be quick in thinking after post-pregnancy because not before long the baby will wake up and stop any of these shenanigans!

Post-baby intimacy is like trying to remember how to drive a car – except the car has been hit by a truck, left out in the rain and you're not even sure if the engine even works anymore. Do you remember, spending those days, weeks building up the courage to even consider reacquainting the birds and the bees? Questions of, 'Is it safe and when is it safe after having a baby?' would run through your mind and most likely be typed into Google. And let's be honest, by the time you even got the green light to get back into the sack your enthusiasm was as lively as the houseplant that you forgot to water for the last six months. The idea of anything physical made you feel like cattle being prodded.

But there will always be that one member of the Mum Squad who swears she can't wait to get back into the sexual pleasures of Fifty Shades of Post-Baby Sex, and everyone asking her not only if she is ready but where the hell does she find the time and the energy to complete one shade of grey let alone fifty?

So, whether you dived straight back in, took your time or still haven't even thought about it – the logistics of timing and positioning all form part of 'The Road to Motherhood.' If you're still trying to find your spark, you may want to return to the maternity hospital as it may have been left there. One thing is for sure, sex after having children will never be the same and we are not talking body parts, it's the freedom to jump in the sack whenever you want. It's more inhibited, volume down, catch the moment and one ear at the door – unless the kids go to Grandma's.

The Hormone Rollercoaster

One minute you are crying over a puppy advert; the next, you are yelling because someone breathed too loudly around you - it's all part of 'The Road to Motherhood,' so hold on tight, the rollercoaster has just begun.

WOMEN HAVE IT HARD when it comes to hormones – don't they? Without us even realising it we are forever on the rollercoaster of hormones throughout our whole lives. First, we hit puberty hormones, then pregnancy and motherhood hormones and then menopausal hormones. No break, just one rollercoaster loop after another. Just like rollercoasters they have their highs, their lows, make you feel like you're going around in circles and make you sick. There is no escaping them, no pretending to hide from them and their effect on every part of you, mind, body and soul. Yes, hormones are the little buggers that work with Sod's Law to come in when you least expect or want them to.

As you know, hormones play havoc with your emotions from the moment you find out you're pregnant and continue after your children are here. There is no escaping them and they will create different sides of your personalities that some people may even give a name. So not only are you juggling being a woman and motherhood, but you are also juggling the hormonal mafia inside of you who are running the show every day. During pregnancy though, these personalities are like the Jekyll and Hyde Mum. You wake up feeling like:

Joyful Jane

Full of smiles and senses of gratitude for a growing bump and the next stage of your life about to spring into action. The smiles at the morning baby bump kicks, scrolling your phone for baby outfits and the sun shining through the window. The Joyful Jane presence lasts all but ten minutes before the next personality makes its appearance.

Queasy Queenie

Just as you think about breakfast Queasy Queenie pushes Joyful Jane out of the sun shining window and makes you feel sick. Really sick. Some of you may have just had the feeling and some of you would have been acquainted with your toilet once again. Queasy Queenie brings her friend along for the show who takes over just when you feel you can't take anymore.

Tearful Tracy

The personality that enters your thoughts and feelings and results in you bursting out into tears. Why is this happening to you? The tears flow over the slightest of thoughts of what you're experiencing, feeling or the fear of what's to come. It's here you're usually consoled by your partner, friend or colleague.

Lovely Lisa

With a beaming heart of comfort and gratitude your next personality pops in to reassure Tearful Tracy that things will be OK. You suddenly want to hug people, show gratitude for them and even be comfortable in sharing a vulnerable moment. The Lovely Lisa personality reminds you that you are loved and have others around you.

Craving Carla

As the sickness passes you begin to feel hungry and then Craving Carla appears to remind you to eat certain foods. Usually, the opposite of what you would normally enjoy, some have the most bizarre cravings. Craving Carla gives you the energetic burst to search the fridge for your supply of your craving snacks only to find that someone has eaten the last one.

Raging Rita

No surprises here when Raging Rita shows up because there is one thing everyone should remember and that is you don't mess with a woman's food supply – pregnant or not! As Raging Rita begins to yell out to find the culprit, she is not in the mood to play games, she wants answers and is out for revenge.

Overthinking Olivia

Amongst the rage that Raging Rita brings there begins to seep a little doubt if you were the one who ate the last craving snack and forgot to top them up. Overthinking Olivia will fill your mind with doubts and will lead you to feeling like you have just shouted at the wrong person.

Scatterbrain Sarah

Now that you have reassured yourself that it is you and not someone else stealing your last craving snack, you are acquainted with Scatterbrain Sarah who makes you realise you are losing your marbles and are forgetting more than ever. Scatterbrain Sarah then shows you all the other things you are forgetting or can't think about to prove to you that baby brain fog is real.

Exhausted Emily

After a run in with more personalities than you can keep track of, Exhausted Emily pops in to give you time as the whole experience of these hormones is making you feel tired, and it is only noon. Time for a nap before the rest of the hormonal mafia come in to pay a visit.

You are most likely not only remembering the hormone personalities that motherhood created but realising you are still being acquainted with them today. There is one hormone that has its benefits and that is the one responsible for 'nesting.' Every mum-to-be has their moment of nesting just like little birds gathering their twigs to build the nest for their awaited little offspring. And right now, you are wishing that nesting energy would return as you have a whole load of household chores to do and plenty of cupboards to clear. The nesting energy that caused you to clean in ways you have never done before. Cleaning in the most bizarre and perhaps not so safe ways – nesting forgot to remind you that you had a growing bump in front of you. From standing on side cabinets, legs apart to reach and clean the top window, to cleaning the bath with so much limescale cleaning products that you take off the enamel. Then there are the women who have that urge to break down wardrobes to create more space. No matter what, the nesting hormone just got the job done.

So, there we have the hormonal rollercoaster that can leave you feeling far from a Disney princess and more like Princess Fiona, transforming overnight into a raging ogre.

The Final Push (Literally)

Birth plans are great, but as you know babies don't read them.

DIGNITY. SOMETHING YOU ONCE had but was left inside the labour ward along with the gown they provided that for some reason hospital staff still ask you to change into yet half of it is missing – leaving you to decide if your front or back is going to be on show because no one ever shows you how to put them on correctly.

As you left the labour ward you not only left with a baby but also a memory. The memory of that final push. For those of you who were numb or had a C-section, just imagine your vagina being on fire and you will picture the pain. There is no dignified experience of giving birth regardless of how you brought your baby into this world. Your dignity went right out of the window the moment your vagina took centre stage and became the main event for every person passing the room to stop and take a glare at. Back then, you never even questioned your dignity in that moment, in fact you opened your legs more times than ever just to find out how far your labour had progressed.

What none of us women ever question at the time or even now, is the measuring technique used to decide how far you have progressed during labour. The long-anticipated measurement that can send a woman into turmoil when you realise how far you still have left to go. Each stage measured by centimetres, no rulers or gadgets involved, simply the hand of each midwife who measured you. But what if you had a midwife with small or large fingers? The miscalculation of even a half of a centimetre would have made the difference from you being sent home for not yet being in established labour to not yet ready to push. Not one of us questioned the measurements – and should a male doctor with big hands come into the measuring process we have literally tipped all odds that these measurements were correct in the first place. Now you are probably sizing up your own fingers to see if each one represents a centimetre or not.

Looking back, it is kind of comical how the whole birth experience is mapped out in our birthing plans but is a complete contrast to what actually happens in there. All these trained midwives and health professionals who know exactly what goes on inside those labour rooms, handed you once a piece of paper and encouraged you to write a birth plan. A plan that made you feel empowered and in control, all of which makes you feel a little delusional especially if you were one of the women who wanted soft sounding music playing and a hypno-birth but ended up shouting and swearing at the music and everyone in the room.

What the hospital staff forgot to tell you was that your birthing plan didn't correspond to the anaesthetist's staffing rota so any hope of getting an epidural depended on their shift pattern and how busy the ward would be. In fact, if you had known this you would have brought in a packed lunch for them, so they had no excuse to not be available whilst you were having contractions. Sod's Law comes into play in whatever happened inside that room. Birthing plans have their place and when they work out, fabulous, but when they don't you will feel it was the biggest pile of crap and time wasted in completing one. They should have come with a disclaimer on how many actually pan out the way the women hoped because every woman you speak to you never had a tick box birth plan that went accordingly to how they hoped. I mean, who would write on their birthing plan, 'Request to repair my vagina back into place please.'

C-section mums have their own questions when comparing their scars to other women – maybe the size of the scar they are left with depends on the size of the hands of the doctor who delivered their baby. So much depends on hands and fingers in this delivery operation that no one has a method to this madness.

The amount of effort and time you put into preparing for that one moment is kind of comical looking back. The months of your midwife encouraging you to make decisions which felt right for you, you colour coding the sequence of delivery so that it made is easier to follow and then creating a music playlist to be played to 'set the mood' – have you ever looked back on the playlist you created to 'set the mood' for the delivery and thought you were one naive woman who would have replaced the rainfall droplets with songs like Meat Loaf's Bat Out of Hell? Where on earth did the aromatherapy oils keep you calm? More like the gas and air did. The polite phrase of, 'Please rub my back,' was more like, 'Come near me again and I will bite you.' It wasn't just dignity that transformed back then, no, your whole tolerance to people telling you to 'just breathe' disappeared too.

As for the antenatal classes preparing you for birth – did they actually? Really think about this. Did they actually prepare you for all the different positions that you would need to try? From giving birth on all fours resembling an animal, crouching down, and squatting to having your legs up in stirrups – no there was no preparation for this and definitely not once did they show you how to put those hospital gowns on. No wonder women who have had a baby never return to the classes after their second. Yes, they have their uses, especially the controlled breath work, but from painting the picture of expectations versus reality – it was the lesson they forgot to include.

There will be a cheerful moment from the adults inside the room when the midwife declares the 'crowning' moment that can make your sub-conscious compare it to the coronation of a king or queen. There was no crown involved, no, just the feeling you were on fire down there and everyone telling you to pant like a dog on heat. The whole experience should have come with the theme tune of Johnny Cash's 'Ring of Fire' playing in the background to add more comical elements to this very unexpected sequence of events that your birth plan seemed to be missing a page to prepare you for this. Seriously, crowning and ring of fire are completely two different experiences as you fully well know if you had a vaginal birth.

Did you find that the moment you were ready to push you began to focus on everyone's face inside the room as they seemed to be all taking the centre VIP standing area in staring at your vagina? The disappointing look and sighs in the room as you pushed, and you hear, 'The head is there – oh no it's gone again,' as the baby goes back again. How helpful was this? It was enough to frustrate you and feel the need to hand popcorn out to the spectators whilst they forgot the fire happening down there. Then there were the midwives who shouted, 'Push like you need to go to the toilet!' It certainly doesn't feel like any toilet experience you have had before.

Now whilst some of you are playing with the ring of fire and fearing splitting yourself into two, there are other women who deliver via C-section. Just because they don't have to deliver the watermelon in the same way, it certainly isn't a, 'sit back and relax' kind of experience. They will have had to endure someone digging around in their stomach which would have felt like someone was washing up in there. If you delivered by C-section, you would of course have the after recovery which had its own challenges and sneezing moments that you would rather forget.

So whatever way you deliver your bundle of joy you will not only be greeted by a tiny human but the comment from your partner who tells you that you look so beautiful. If you had a mirror in that moment, you would notice your hair was everywhere, sweat pulling your make-up off, red faced and knackered. Of all the comments, 'beautiful' does not feel the appropriate thing to say right now. As much as you would usually welcome this comment and it would probably lead to another night of passion, you shake your head and give a sigh of relief that it is over with.

The Birth Story Lottery

The only lottery where the prize is a tiny human and a complete loss of dignity.

Y OU PROBABLY HAD MORE chances of predicting a lottery win than what kind of birth you would have had. Even after the first birth, there is still no indication of what would have come next for your second and so on births. Sod's Law played its role here too, letting you know it held all the cards and all you could do was hope that mother nature was kind to you. As for due dates, you know only too well that it is like a game of bingo. Sitting there waiting for that number to be called exactly when you need it to, only to find it either came out too early or too late. Yes, due dates are the lucky charm if your child is ever born on that exact date, but most likely due dates would have left you holding your breath in anticipation if that was the day you would experience the birth story from hell. Yes, there was excitement to see the baby but by the time you got to the due date and looked down at your stomach in full bloom, you just couldn't work out how the hell you were going to deliver a baby of that size.

The moment you went into labour you entered the lottery draw once again, but this time in hope that your own birth story was not like any of the other stories that had been shared with you. As you clutched onto your birthing plan, your maternity notes and a bag that had been repacked several times, you headed for the labour ward the moment the first twinge started. It was a time of transition, you knew the moment you entered there was no going back, you had to see this mission through and you secretly whispered to Sod's Law to sod off this time and leave you alone because all you wanted was to leave with your vagina intact and a story to share that gave hope that delivering a baby is not like every story you hear.

Head held high, dignity still intact and a room full of calmness. Your first experience was full of anticipation, the second time and so on will always be full of knowing what is to come and hoping to get the deed over with as quickly as possible – but this time you have an A-Z chart of all the drugs you are allowed ready to express your demands the moment the contractions begin. Second time mums and so on are ready for this mission, especially if their last birth was a horror story. There is no way they are going back.

So, there you are, lottery balls back in play with your delivery fate sealed and no chance of an escape plan – your baby must come out one way or another. Maybe you hit the jackpot and was the woman of labour breeze or perhaps Sod's Law entered the room, and it was the labour from hell or C-section surprise.

Either way, you now have a labour story or two to share of your own and hold the cape of the women below:

Horror Birth Holly

Credentials – The first time Mum with the birth that was opposite to what was written on the plan.

From the moment the bump arrives right up to the delivery room, Horror Birth Hollys look like they have everything under control but secretly feel the fear of what will happen the moment the baby is on the way. They plan, prep, listen to what to do and what not to do, they feel in control until Sod's Law becomes their extra birthing partner and shows them that no matter what they plan it can be tipped upside down because they had the birth from hell. Yes, everything women wish not to experience they do. From being prodded, poked, and torn, the Horror Birth Hollys wear the cape for their honorary strength that they upheld in the delivery room. Usually, it is their first rodeo, and they will let everyone know soon after birth that it will be their last. They will share their story with pregnant mums to be in some way to warn them but also to process the traumatic experience that the birth room brought to them. The blood, sweat and tears, their faces will show it all and it will be a horror story like no movie ever seen before.

Breeze Birth Bella

Credentials – The woman who won the birth lottery and everything went smoothly and had minimal impact on her vagina.

Now, Breeze Birth Bellas are the rare birth experiences, the jackpot winners and the ones who manage to survive the whole experience with minimal pain and impact. They have this kind of amnesia when it comes to their own experience of birth, and usually this is because they are topped up with as much pain relief as they can get their hands on. Everything happens so quickly that the whole experience is actually 'not as bad as they thought.'

Honestly these are the rarest of births and other women will look up in amazement at their story. There will be no mention of repairs which will leave your imagination wondering if they have a bucket crutch or the baby's head was the smallest of them all. The downside of being a Breeze Birth Bella is that there is always that fear that next time they might not be so lucky and the pretence that they have everything under control fades very quickly on their next pregnancy. These women spend the whole of their next pregnancy dreading that they may have just been the 'lucky' one at the time and waiting for others to say, 'I told you so.'

Naturelle Birth Natalie

Credentials – Research specialist to the 'T' and birthing plan master minder.

With these little professors inside the birthing room, you tend to find fear drives their research to find the most natural ways to deliver their baby so that they can stay in control. They tend to cover up their concerns with scientific strategies, research and plenty of natural theories that are certainly guaranteed to work for them. These little superheroes have their whole birthing experience natural, no pain relief, everything calm and collective. The sound of soft music playing and calmness within the room with no intervention is the perfect birth for Naturelle Birth Natalies of the motherhood world. But they do have two sides to them. The sweet, under control and pleasant planned experience can create images of butterflies and rainbows but when they suddenly realise this birth experience is not what was planned, things begin to turn ugly... very ugly.

They start with the tightness of their hand grip and then the clenching of their teeth, every bit of calmness goes out of the window with their dignity. This once carefree and birth planning expert now wants to become friends with the local drug dealer. You guessed it, they don't know how, where or what drugs they want, 'You just have to get them.' As their birth partners try to reason with them, they won't listen. They glare into their eyes and words of, 'Get me drugs and more drugs,' makes the people around them fear with dread that this birth experience has unleashed the next friend of the local drug dealer. The funny story here is that after the birth, these mums will laugh at this and laugh at how they wanted to rip up and tear the birthing plan in front of the damn person who suggested it.

Section Specialist Suzie

Credentials – The C-Section Licensed Expert in Overcoming the 'Don't Laugh or Sneeze' Challenge.

Section Specialist Suzies of the motherhood world tend to not have birthing experiences that go to plan. They end up having to go into full operation planning mode – whether the C-section was planned or not. After birth they will remind you that it is all, 'as it should be' down there, not always to gloat, but to remind themselves how fortunate they are… until they laugh, cough or sneeze. When this happens, prepare yourself to be amazed, and of course laugh as you will never see anything else quite like it again. You will witness manoeuvres that you didn't even realise were possible. One small sneeze will feel like their stomach is being pulled in every direction. This is the moment vaginal birth mothers become grateful that they are not having to try out for the next gymnastics competition of who can bend the most.

And there you have it, the birth lottery stories. Looking back now, we can laugh at moments where we screamed, shouted, said the craziest things under gas and air but we all share that one thing in common – first labour is a shock, second labour deja-vu, and third labour you will be just wanting to get the job done and get back for school pick-up hours.

Congratulations, It's Chaos!

Nothing prepares you for the first few weeks with a newborn - except maybe the equivalent of running a marathon whilst assembling flat pack furniture on zero hours sleep.

THERE IS NOTHING QUITE like those first few weeks of holding your baby and staring at them, questioning, 'Are you really mine?' It is the most surreal moment of all time. Until the moment all the chaos begins. Congratulations, welcome to motherhood! There is no preparation for it, no adjustments, just straight into motherhood and everything as you know it changes around you. It is like being thrown into the deep end of a swimming pool without aids or any knowledge of how to swim. You even check the labels in the baby's clothing in the hope that there is a hidden manual or set of instructions on how to raise this little human. But no, there is no manual, no instructions, just a baby that you are responsible for from thereon in and a whole heap of expectations from society on how to do a bloody good job in raising them otherwise your mum status would be compromised.

As you looked around your home, not realising it was the last time you would see calmness and tidiness in the same way ever again, well for at least the next eighteen years. You took a sigh of relief looking forward to sitting on your backside on the sofa for the foreseeable, then it happened... the doorbell rang and as you opened the door to the first set of visitors, you opened the door to the chaos that followed. There was no going back, you had well and truly entered 'The Road to Motherhood.'

Did You Forget About the Poo Explosions?

There were many moments of chaos that stopped you in your tracks and you had no choice but to handle them, sometimes swearing under your breath wishing someone had warned you beforehand and these things could have been prevented – such as making damn sure the nappy was secured on both sides. But no, they wanted you to experience it yourself. The 'learning' came after a poo explosion that not only covered your baby, but you too. The worst of its kind where everything needs to be removed, you guessed it, Sod's Law brought this little surprise to you at 3am. In fact, every time you tried to leave the house on time, visit family or go out for the day. The poo chaos that stopped you in your tracks, made you heave and showed you that you were never in control no matter how well prepared you were. As you held your baby's legs up like a little strung chicken whilst you tried to clear up an avalanche that hadn't quite finished.

Babies' nappies should have a red warning label on them that is for sure and the moment you finally had everything under control was just in time for the next round of pooping – they never seemed to stop. Being covered in poop, snot and food was like earning your motherhood stripes – without it you haven't had the real experience of chaos – and it really isn't something you would have forgotten but you did try to.

Did They Really Need That Much Milk?

Did you breastfeed? If you did you would have felt like Daisy the cow, constantly feeling like one boob was out all the time feeding the demands of your little human. Your once lovely, perfect perked boobs were being filled and expressed more times than a cow's udders and no one prepared you for the chaos of the sore nipples that followed. Yes, breastfeeding is good for the baby, but they forgot to mention, 'but may feel sore for you.' Suddenly, your once perfectly ripened plums, apples, melons, depending on your cup size, that once looked fabulous in a push up bra, were simply transferred into feeding machines, with the boobs coming in and out like a yoyo.

Or did you bottle feed? If so, you may have felt you had it easier than breastfeeding mummies as you could get others to help with the feeding, but, and there is a big BUT, you had an additional job – the milk production line to prepare for each feed.

Sterilising bottles and scooping out powder before cooling the milk down – which always felt like forever. No matter how cold the tap was, the milk still stayed warm. Yes, demand feeding babies don't like to wait for milk to be cooled. The tears and screams grew louder and louder because when babies want their milk there is no concept of patience. You would talk to the water to ask it to hurry up and for some reason you really thought it would. Sod's Law set the baby off crying to remind you it was feeding time just as you were about to get settled. Bottle feeding needed a routine on its own from sterilising, preparing, and getting the bottle ready for the next feed. Then there are the fussy babies who don't like the teats or the bottle shape, babies who seem to develop the fussy gene immediately from birth. I mean, breastfed babies don't demand a new nipple, do they? No, they must get used to it. But bottle-fed babies are the stubborn babies when it comes to teats they don't like.

When it comes down to feeding, the difference between popping out a boob and preparing a bottle was left down to each of you to decide what was right for you. Either way, yes, they did need all that milk and certainly disposed of it at the other end!

What Was Sleep?

Back in your party and clubbing days, staying up all night or to at least to 4am was easy. But the moment you hit 'The Road to Motherhood' sleep becomes so precious. You can't function without it. You can't imagine how you danced the night away yet found it so difficult to wake up for a feed.

You will recall that babies and sleep don't go hand in hand and their little lungs are the loudest alarm clocks you will have ever come to know. The moment you put your baby down or close your eyes, they will have this sense, which is stronger than any other sense you know, and they will remind you they are there. You would have tried all the tricks from slowly prising them from your arms, to swaddling, holding their little finger – anything just to get a moment of sleep. Then it happened. Out of nowhere, just as you and your baby were settled for the night you SNEEZED. Yes, not only were you dealing with the sneeze but the manoeuvres of holding your vagina bits together to free yourself from pain. That was it. You would hold your breath and legs together in hope the baby missed that sound, but no, the shuffling began, and the little cry started. You had woken up the baby and had to start the mission all over again! It wasn't only the sneezes, during the day it could be the phone, the doorbell, other children in the house or outside, neighbours or an ambulance passing by – your baby was fitted with a sound detector that alerted them at the slightest of sounds.

They told you to sleep when the baby slept but no one ever tells you what to do when you already have children. Sleep as a mother of a newborn is near impossible and matchsticks become your best friend – and coffee if you can remember to drink it and not have to keep reheating it!

How Many Visitors?

Visitors, whether you loved them or hated them – you had plenty of them. There is never a better time to visit someone than welcoming a new baby. When the word got out you that the baby had arrived home, the visitors gathered. Very rarely did they plan their visits and your house felt more like an open house with the doorbell going every five minutes. Just as you washed the mugs away, the kettle went back on to refill them again for your next lot of visitors. Eventually the visiting chaos came to an end, after what felt like an endless open house party for your bundle of joy. You were left with so many gifts that could have filled a gift shop, a fridge of cooked food, and your sanity hanging by a thread. But you did it, you survived the newborn visitor invasion with 200 photographs added to your phone. With a heart full of gratitude, you blissfully sighed knowing the visitors had all been and gone and it was time for you to rest – until the messages began for their next visiting requests.

When Did Supermarket Trips Become a Mission Impossible?

The moment you entered motherhood, gone were the days when you could just collect your bags and head to the car for the weekly shop. No, from the moment of delivery, there were no more supermarket sweeps, in fact it became supermarket missions. You would need to plan them out in hope it would be your baby's nap time, although they would always have other plans. There you were having to pack a bag that contained EVERYTHING that you could possibly need 'just in case.' The whole planning and packing were more effort than you have ever done in packing for a holiday. On top of this, you would often forget what shopping you needed – the baby brain is real and most of us still have it years on! Sod's Law would come on the supermarket trip with you and give your baby a nudge for the changing or feeding act to commence right in the middle of the aisle or at the checkout – it would never be at the beginning or end of your visit. Food shopping was never the same again.

Housework and Babies – How Did We Manage That Then?

Somewhere between the feeding, the changing, trying to remember what day it was, there was something else that needed our attention. The housework. Seriously, how on earth did we all manage to fit that in whilst trying to navigate a newborn? Even trying to change the perspective from a tidy home to now owning a 'lived in' home. You had to come to terms with the fact that your once neat and tidy home was no more and that a little human had taken over the whole home. If you squinted your eyes it would look 'lived in' but from the eye of anyone else, it was more like a disaster zone – and you would always have that one visitor who noticed. Washing piling up, floors needing to be mopped, all the endless jobs that there just wasn't the time for. When we did get on top of it, the whole cycle started again.

So, what did that all result in? It resulted in us joining the mama silly hour o'clock. The eleventh hour of the evening when others were off to bed, we would widen our eyes and tackle the load. This was when you wished your nesting hormone phase had stayed as it would have never taken you that long back then. Your new mantra became 'a lived-in home, is a family home' – it helped on the nights when you truly couldn't stay awake past 10pm.

Despite the chaos of those early days, you somehow survived the sleepless nights, endless feeding, endless pooping, and entertained visitors galore – all while clinging to your sanity. You did it. You got through the chaos and lived to tell the tale. And one day, you'll even laugh about it… because when people tell others to get the baby into a routine, you know only too well that babies and routine don't go hand in hand.

The Mum Squad

Every mum needs a group of women to stop her from going insane, to wipe the tears and bring the wine.

'THE ROAD TO MOTHERHOOD' would not be complete without the Mum Squad being behind you every step of the way. The friends you didn't think you would meet, but did, and the friends you didn't want to let go of – and in some cases could not get rid of. Yes, the Mum Squad is full of women who themselves have entered 'The Road to Motherhood' and all share their expertise with you from their own journeys. Sometimes offering unsolicited advice, without invitation to help you ease into the chaos as it unfolded. Their job was to fully support you hand in hand so that you were never alone. As you know the only problem with the Mum Squad is that their overarching support could sometimes be a little overwhelming which led you to hiding behind trees in the park and leaving phone messages unread to pretend you just haven't seen them.

When you first entered 'The Road to Motherhood' you convinced yourself that you did not need any more friends, especially women who talked non-stop about nappies, baby routines and how sleep deprived they were. This was not your thing – you would have rather watched paint dry then get stuck into those conversations. All you wanted back then was to ease into motherhood and still have your usual girly night hangouts and have adult conversations away from the baby talk. As much as you may have wanted this, there was a huge part of you that was in denial that you really needed the Mum Squad in your life. From the moment you became a mum, you somehow developed this beaming light above your head that attracted other mums to draw you in. Every walk you took, women with babies would approach you for conversations, coffee invites and share stories of their motherhood moments. You couldn't even hide from these women; they were everywhere and seemed to multiply in numbers the more your baby grew.

Just because you became a mum didn't mean you were the next neighbourhood best friend to all the women out there. It felt like you were in a motherhood trap every time you left the house. Ducking, diving and hiding away from the magnet of mothers waving for your attention. All you did was have a baby and then somehow entered a motherhood cult. Just when you thought you didn't need the Mum Squad in your life – the inevitable happens. You realise your existing child-free friends don't understand your woes and stresses. The friends who you would once reach out to for relationship advice suddenly went green in the face the moment you mention a cracked nipple or how to get baby vomit out of the sofa. The world of motherhood did not exist for them, but it did for you – and there were plenty of reminders around you. There was the sudden realisation that you can longer hold your sanctity together and needed support from a Mum Squad.

Welcome to the Mum Squad. You can find us in:

The Coffee Shops

Coffee shops are the hangout of new mums. Babies sleep whilst each mum would gather for a coffee and talk about the motherhood chaos. The moment you stepped into the coffee shop a seat was already waiting for you. Before you knew it, your conversation flowed, connections were built and phone numbers for your new Mum Squad network had been shared. You left the coffee shop with your head held high, a sigh of relief that you had been heard and a reminder from a leaking boob that it was just about feeding time. Yes, there is nothing like a reminder that you no longer own dignity then seeing a milk stain on your top as you breeze through the spring day without a jacket to cover up. It didn't matter, you were part of a Mum Squad and things like this happened.

The Baby Groups

Once you were in full swing of the motherhood meet-ups it was only right to seek out your local baby groups and become a regular member. As you sat in a circle, all singing and lifting your babies and smiling across the circle at each other, you had a moment where you wondered what the hell happened to that once polished city woman whose only connection to the floor was at her Pilates lesson. Gone were the satisfying days of cocktails with your friends and talking about world politics and how cute the guy was sitting over on the next table. Sitting in this circle was the only reminder you needed that motherhood had a world of its own. But these women understood you. They shared the same frustrations as you. You had finally found your Mum Squad tribe where you belonged.

So, meet the Mum Squad who you became acquainted with; some remain acquaintances and others still loyal friends today.

The Supermum

These members are mums on speed doing everything and anything for their children with no challenge too small or too big. Before 10am, they have their routines for the day underway, meals prepared and looking fabulous. The Supermums are the leaders who women look up to in hope they will share their wisdom on how to juggle it all.

The Hot Mess Mum

Her mission alone is to survive the day with a happy, fed and changed baby. She won't remember where she left her keys, which bag the nappies were in or what to buy in the supermarket once she arrived there. The Hot Mess mums are there to show the world of women that they don't have their sh*t together and don't give a sh*t what you think either. Survival is the key and wine will be needed by the end of the week.

The Motherhood Guru

The go-to experts for nappy rash, weaning, and how to repair your pelvic floor. These Motherhood Guru mums have read all the baby books, spent hours on Google and survive on caffeine – so buying them a coffee is a must in return for their advice. The Motherhood Gurus are the mums you can rely on at 2am to text, 'Why is my baby still crying?'

The Motherhood Rebel

Whatever she has been told she will do the opposite. She lives life in the moment with no routine, no plan and puts her fingers up to any kind of expectations. Yes, defying every 'should do' with 'won't do.' The Motherhood Rebels are the ones handing out tequila shots at the next Mum Squad night out. Motherhood may have defined them, but it has also unleashed a new side of them.

The Newbie

Approaching each group meet up with a zombie look from lack of sleep, still waddling from their bruised vagina that delivery left her with and holding it all together, just waiting for the validation that she is doing OK. The Newbie mums are wanting the most support from the Mum Squad because 'The Road to Motherhood' has more chaos then they ever thought. She wants reassurance and lots of it!

The Realist

Don't you just love the mums who tell you how it is and as they open their mouths you laugh not at them but at the courage they have to say what they mean. Yes, the realist mums are the mums who leave their conversations unfiltered, honest in their actions, even if it means she admits that 'Love Island' keeps her baby entertained whilst she gets a minute's peace. These Mum Squad members don't care what reactions they receive; they do what they want because they make it work for them. They don't suck up all the rainbows and fluffy clouds talk – they keep it real and encourage you to do it your way.

So here is to your own Mum Squad friendship group, the women who have seen you at your worst, picked you up from your meltdowns and showed up with coffee and cake, lots of sarcasm when needed because you couldn't get more honest friends than them! Your Mum Squad, forever keeping it real, helping you keep it together and never telling a soul what they really know about you!

And this concludes the first part of 'The Road to Motherhood.' I look forward to you joining me for the next part of the journey.

But there is one thing left and that is to hear from the men... because no matter what they say, 'It takes two to tango,' and even though you are the one carrying the watermelon, your partner is on his own journey from the moment you see those two lines.

So welcome to 'The Road to Fatherhood.' If your partner had written this book, this would be his version!

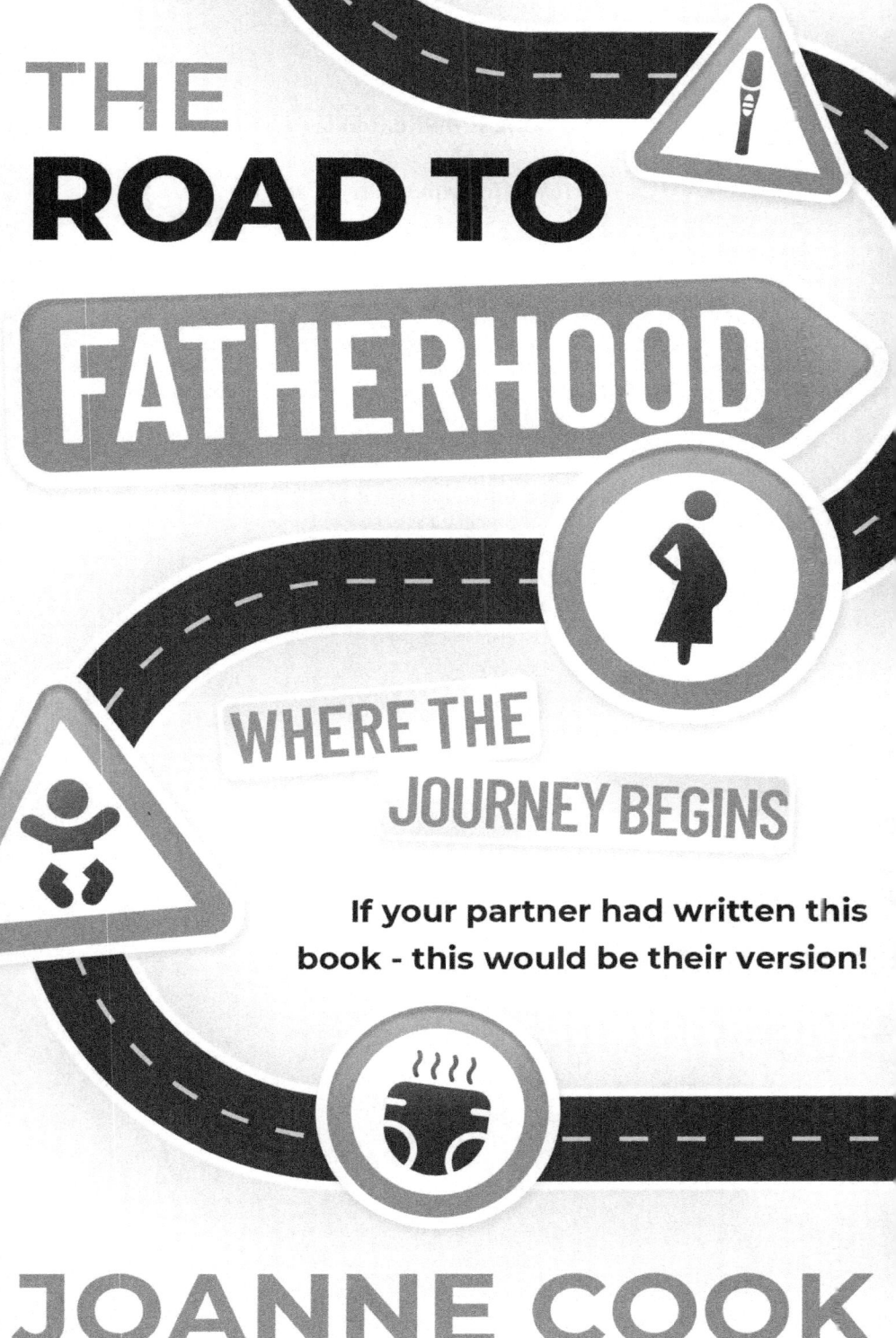

This book is dedicated to:

To My Husband, Terry

Thank you for walking beside me on 'The Road to Motherhood' even while finding your own way through 'The Road to Fatherhood.' We did it together and what a wonderful job we have done in raising both Jack and Billy to become the amazing men they are today.

I couldn't ask for a better partner to share my life with. Thank you for always believing in me and helping me to make this book series happen.

Love you for eternity.

The Road to Fatherhood: Where it Begins

THERE ARE OVER FOUR billion women in this world, yet as men none of us will ever really understand any one of them – no matter how much we try. The only thing that we will ever understand is the blame game.

Whether you are to blame or not, it will be your fault and yours alone – no matter how many times you are in the right, it still won't be accepted. There are so many books on pregnancy, motherhood and even fatherhood, but there is no book written by a woman that actually helps us men understand the female species. If there is such a book, it must be hidden somewhere in fear of us opening it to find the blank pages – because they probably don't even know how to explain the thousands of emotions they experience, let alone write about them.

So, to all fathers out there on 'The Road to Fatherhood' – welcome to the blame game.

They will blame us men for feeling heavy and uncomfortable from being pregnant – even though they were part of the act too.

They will blame us for not understanding their emotions – even though they change how they feel every five minutes.

They will blame us for not telling them to do something the right way after a mishap – even though we did, but they didn't want our advice.

The blame game is a game that no man will ever win.

As you embark on this book series, you will be wishing that you had read these books before you first became a dad and reliving some of those moments when you really did put your foot in it. 'The Road to Fatherhood' has just as many bumps, roundabouts, and diversions as 'The Road to Motherhood' – even though the Mum Squad will tell you that it doesn't.

Don't worry, we have got you and this book series will take you back to reflecting on each step of 'The Road to Fatherhood' – the moments of joy, the birth room shenanigans and the curiosity that got the better of you – and landed you in a load of trouble with your other half. You will feel like someone truly understood you and your journey.

Welcome to 'The Road to Fatherhood.'

Two Lines

The moment she tells you she's pregnant... that's your cue to smile, nod, and quietly Google how to take out a second mortgage!

THE MOMENT TWO LINES are declared on a pee stick, it is shoulders back and chin up, time to rise to the challenge, followed by a quick stop at the pub to absorb the words you've just heard, 'It's positive.' Two beers later and one word solidifies the journey you're about to begin...

'The Road to Fatherhood.'

Have you ever noticed that everything is complicated on 'The Road to Motherhood?' Even the simplest of tasks like peeing on a stick is more complicated than it should be. When women open the test packet, the instructions clearly state what to do, but no, they spend the next thirty minutes in the toilet still trying to read the instructions because apparently, they are not clear. Seriously, just pee on the stick and get it done – what is complicated about that? Once they have peed on the stick, the positive reveal follows and in the hands of every woman on how she is going to break the news to you:

Exiting the Toilet Reveal

If you are outside the toilet, you probably know she is in there taking the pee stick test. You wait outside anticipating and wondering why it is taking so long when the instructions said a result will appear in five minutes. As she opens the door you then enter a game of Catchphrase trying to guess the result from her face. Women have this distinctive look on their face leaving you dreading what they are going to say. Their eyes glare and their features are hard to read, leaving you wondering what exactly this pee stick revealed. After a few moments of pausing, the positive result is revealed. Whether your response is a big, 'YES', 'Oh sh*t!' or 'Seriously, it can't be,' – you are on 'The Road to Fatherhood.' Welcome on board and to the world of responsibility!

The Car Reveal

As you get ready to pull away from the kerb, she turns to you and says, 'I have something to tell you.' Followed by the longest pause ever, leaving you wondering why she has a serious look on her face. Thoughts running through your mind in what it could possibly be and then she hits you with the big reveal. Whether your response is full of excitement, full of horror or shock you will just be glad it wasn't one of the thoughts that you were thinking of. Welcome to 'The Road to Fatherhood' and eighteen years of responsibility!

The Text Message Reveal

When you receive a text message that reads, 'I need to talk to you,' from a woman you only met once and that was over four weeks ago, it can only mean two things – she has either gained something or given you something. Panic sets in and you reply, 'Sure.' with your fate in her reveal when you meet up. The moment you hear the news; it's game over and all you can think about is what your mum is going to say. Not because you're a mummy's boy but because she told you enough times to be careful and you didn't listen. The questions flow and you're now bonded with a woman you once met in a club and had the best night of passion with, but you can't remember her name – how are you going to approach that after the news? Either way, welcome to 'The Road to Fatherhood.'

The Christmas Present Box Reveal

As the gifts from the tree are given out after Christmas lunch, with all the extended family waiting to see what gifts they get to open, you are given a boxed gift from your excited partner. As you go to open it, she stops you abruptly because she wants everyone to look on. Wondering what she has bought you and secretly hoping it is a key to a Bentley, you are surprised to see a pee stick test which is positive. She screams with delight and waits for your reaction – the next minutes will terminate your New Year's celebrations that's for sure. Everyone is waiting. Come on – are you happy, shocked or scared? Whatever it is, welcome to 'The Road to Fatherhood.'

Whatever the result, whether you planned it or not, us men all dread the instant responsibility these two lines bring. We enjoyed doing the deed and now we are reaping the aftermath that we never even thought about that night. For each of us one word follows the reveal except for the, 'Who's the daddy?' men who have lots of questions as they can't believe they hit the target the first time. What women don't get is why us men celebrate our fast little swimmers, our pride and joy, working to their fullest potential but also eliminating years of secretly worrying that they may not be swimmers after all. Even the 'Who's the daddy?' men celebrate their successful implantation with a big cheer whilst yelling, 'I've got a hole in one!' The 'Who's the daddy?' men have double celebration here for not only having the fastest swimming but for hitting the bullseye on the first try – their ego is on fire right now!

Fruits of Labour

Her body is changing, her emotions are all over the place, and your job is simple: never, ever, comment on the size of anything!

THERE WILL BE MOMENTS throughout 'The Road to Fatherhood' that will seem like you're a rabbit in headlights and other times you're reading the wrong signals, and it will all be your fault regardless. As your partner's body begins to develop into a fruit bowl with her naming each part of her body with a different fruit you will be in the wrong if you notice the changes and in the wrong if you don't – it's down to you to pick your wrong but be warned neither have a happy ending.

You Admire the Growing Bump

You will simply comment on your partner's bump getting big now. To which they will reply with a burst of tears and sarcastically thank you for pointing out they have put weight on and now presume you find them unattractive. However, if you don't comment, they will ask you how the hell you could miss a bump the size of a watermelon and ask if you take notice of them at all.

You Admire Their Larger Than Normal Breasts

As you go to give them a cuddle you point out how big their boobs are getting. To which your partner will respond with a look of hate and remind you they are not in the mood for any of your suggestions for a night of passion and it was looking at her boobs that got you both into this pregnancy. However, if you don't comment, they will tell all their friends you no longer look at them in the same way as you would always notice the increase in their boob size and feel that you've gone off them.

You Support Them Going Through Piles

You really feel for their uncomfortable rear end drama and seek support from others to find a cure or to bring comfort to them. As you explain to your partner that your boss suggested you buy a particular cream from the pharmacist, she will immediately shut the conversation down and remind you her grapes are her business not your boss's. She will also question what else you are freely discussing about her body to your boss? However, if you don't comment you won't care, as simple as that, and will never understand the pain she is in – sarcastically telling you not to worry about her.

What They Forgot to Tell You

One life, one very different reality to what you thought fatherhood would be like!

ONE OF THE MAGICAL moments in The Road to Fatherhood is the moment you see your baby on the screen at a scan, it really is special. It is the time where fear slips away for a moment, and you find a tear in your eye that you really are going to be a daddy. As you stare at the screen in admiration of your baby being presented to you, you begin to ask questions – lots of them.

What is that? What is this? Is that a …? You simply can't work out the image, you are told it is your baby, but it looks like a potato – are you really the only one seeing a potato? It can't be a baby. Is that what you think you've just seen? Looks like it's a boy. Yes, that is a boy, and he takes after his daddy in that area – go on son! Oops, that cheer in the room will not be welcomed, and you should be prepared to be silenced with just a look from all concerned. Eyes back on the screen, keep still and keep your mouth closed. A potato boy it must be, as you try to take an even closer look to confirm.

No one ever spoke about how magical these scans were and how many exciting buttons there were to press inside the hospital room. I mean controlling the bed going up and down before the doctor came in was the most fun you had in a year. No one ever talks about these moments, but you would have ten kids if they would let you back into that room again for its mechanics.

Other things they forgot to tell you:

The Expense of a Baby Shower

The time goes by so quickly and you feel like every weekend there is something you need to do or go out and buy, that is until the last couple of months where it seems the women keep gathering like little chicks underneath mother hen's wings. They celebrate everything even before the baby is here.

The baby shower you dare not question the costs as it is necessary apparently, but only for women. Why didn't anyone tell you about the cost of a baby shower? You would have saved up for this moment. The cost of the whole baby shower event would have paid for all the baby items in their lifetime. There is something changing within her too as she plans this all-out event of the year. There are parcels being delivered and sent back because they are not the right shade of colour, the cake becomes so grand that she can't find a cake baker to fulfil her wish. The outfit, that is something all the men should stay clear of – this is where the body changing comments seriously can go wrong. The Mum Squad can deal with that one, keep out of it as it will be a safer option.

At this point in the pregnancy not only have you learned to accept you are always in the wrong but also to agree and keep quiet and just pay for what she wants. Messing up the baby shower with a 'How much are you spending?' comment, will apparently leave the poor baby with a memory that their father didn't want the best for them. It's a party not a medical procedure!

The Amount of Time They Get Off to Have a Baby

It is not long before she goes on maternity leave and the countdown is a frustrating part for us men. Yes, her body is changing but we are parents too and don't get the extended holiday off from work. No, if you're lucky you may get two weeks off but not everyone does or had done in the past. Us men must watch our partner open her advent calendar every day in the countdown to the sofa surviving with daytime TV. It really is unfair, and we secretly resent this part of the fatherhood journey but obviously don't tell her that – we will be hit with a list of everything she is going through and will go through, followed by, 'Do you know how hard it will be to return back to work once the baby is here?'

Pregnancy is a time to pick your battles because you won't win them all – probably none of them and two weeks of them turning their back on you in bed.

The Identity Shift

Everywhere you go, when someone that you know, whether that be one of your closest friends or colleagues, they will remind you that you are going to be a dad soon. It is the pre-warning that we need apparently, something which leaves us wondering what this really means for our own identity. They no longer ask, 'Are you going fishing tomorrow?' Becoming a father has big changes in store but one question you had was, 'Will I still get to play on my computer or go out for a lads' night out?'

The Baby Name Battle

When you realise naming your pet was easier than naming a baby - and you had more say in the decision!

Talking of picking your battles, the baby's name battle is the hardest for the fathers. You really must watch women when they pick out a baby's name. They forget what it rhymes with and what the baby's initials represent – they don't take it as seriously as men do.

When it comes to baby names you will be the person who suggests and they will be the person to confirm, although some out there have this rule to simplify it, 'If it's a girl the woman names the baby, if it is a boy, the man names him.' Here is why that doesn't work. If it is a boy, do you honestly think men would get total say over the name? What if we wanted to humour ourselves and call the baby our own name, rather than adding junior to the end of it, we used our name followed by Version 2.0? Or what if we called the baby Buddy – my little Bud? Better still, imagine if the baby was named after a favourite football player, would this be accepted? This is why it can go wrong as, in all honesty, do you honestly believe men would get full responsibility for choosing the name?

Why not keep things simple and call them Dave, I mean everyone knows a Dave and nothing is said about them? Too much time is taken to choose a name that the kid will probably hate anyway and start a long-term name refusal battle where they decide to call themselves by another name. It doesn't need to be complicated, pick a name, any name as long as it doesn't rhyme with fanny, dick or has the initials BJ.

Hump, Bump and a Whole Load of Awkwardness

There's nothing that kills the mood more than the thought two little eyes can see you.

THERE IS ONE THING for sure no matter how eager you were for that moment of passion that started your fatherhood journey, you just can't seem to get over the fact that from now any passion moments will have little eyes on you. Two little eyes of a baby inside, staring at you. It is just wrong and there is no way you will get the thought of these two little eyes out of your mind. It will be a 'no go' moment.

There is another thing us men must consider which women never do. The size of our manhood could hit the baby in these moments of passion. I mean, do the measurements, it's not hard to figure that out. With these thoughts running through your mind, it will be nine months of celibacy. Unless the shape of a pregnant woman is a complete turn on then your eyes and size problem will disappear.

If you do ever get caught in the moment, there will be so many disruptions because apparently it can be very logistical in carrying out the deed. From shoving pillows into gaps, balancing the body, recovering from a cramp and the noises that suddenly appear. Sex before pregnancy is long in the past, moving to life after having children when it really does become a scheduled event that neither you are in the mood for because of the constant interruptions. Good luck, find the time to hump even with a bump if you can but be prepared for a whole lot of awkwardness!

The Hormone Rollercoaster

Her emotions are on a loop: hot, cold, raging thunder and tears of rain - a bit like the British weather, you will never know what to expect each day and everything can change at any moment!

SIT TIGHT AND BUCKLE up for a journey of a rollercoaster of emotions like never before – not yours but hers. You will want her to speak in code every time you come home to pre-empt how she is feeling that day. A greeting of a kiss will be welcomed one day, and another will be the reason she burst into tears. Honestly, the emotions are not just unpredictable but last throughout the whole nine-month journey – and there is no book that can help you to understand either.

All the Men Squad do is shake their head and say, 'We did tell you so,' and put another beer in front of you to share their condolences. As you let it all out and give details on how hard this pregnancy has been on you, the Men Squad will simply nod and agree with everything you say and when you ask for a solution their response will be to simply stay out of her way – but how can you? You want to be there for every part of this journey, so with shoulders back, chin up, you remind yourself of the responsibility and confirm to yourself that you can do this. You will hold it all together and go home to support her. As you turn the key in the door with so much intention of loving support, you receive a look and the words, 'It is your fault.' Back off to the pub you go, the Men Squad were right, it really is the only solution during the rollercoaster emotions. Better still, they have a beer with your name on it, waiting ready for you to return as they have 'been there and done that' before.

The Final Push (Literally)

The place where you will gain a bad back, no sleep, your eating routine out of the window, squeezed privates, and the need to adjust to a whole new reality of the woman you love. Apparently this is what women call 'motherhood?'

When the time came for the birth, it felt so daunting as you didn't know what to expect and it was so hard to see your partner in pain. Every birth is so different, and all you could do was support your partner in the best way you could whilst looking after yourself.

You read the books – well you told her you did – attended the antenatal classes, and practised breathing, even though you knew those classes were a waste of time and they didn't cover any support for fathers going through the birthing experience. You went all in on support and no matter what happened you were the tower of strength. You were reminded time and time again during the delivery that everything was your fault – even though it wasn't, there was no way you were arguing with a woman in labour who began to develop a raging personality you had never seen before.

The Song That Nearly Cost You Your Balls

Have you ever had a song that you just can't get out of your head? Well in the labour room it happens and there is only one song that goes around and around in your mind at the time. It's not your fault that you can't stop singing but just as they start talking of the baby crowning you will suddenly have the lyrics of, 'The Ring of Fire' by Johnny Cash in your head. Once someone mentions it, that's it, you'll be singing along every time she says it burns down there. Seriously, it's not like your partner has never had a song in her head that she can't stop singing. It's not your fault that she is linking the lyrics to her vagina – you never mentioned vagina in the lyrics.

We get called everything inside that room, including being called an insensitive twat. You get told you must never go near her again but a couple of months after she wants to think about planning the next baby. Seriously, they change inside that room and the language they use you have never heard from their mouth before. You only have to say one swear word at home and the look she gives will make you feel like you are back at school in the headteacher's office.

Women are given gas and air to cope during delivery. What do men get? Insults, bite marks and squeezed hands and other body parts. You'll be looking back and thinking 'I'm sure it was her idea that night anyway,' But no, it's your fault... again.

Where Did You Go Darling?

Don't be comparing your sweet and gentle woman who attended the antenatal classes, no this is not the same woman lying on the bed ready to give birth. Gosh, birth will transform her into a swearing, ball squeezing crazy woman. Nights of passion should come with a disclaimer to warn men of this transformation. It's OK, it doesn't last long but when it does you can't even escape the room as they will say you have left them not that they drove you out.

Back Rubbing is Never the Answer

She will want you to rub her back, then not to rub her back. Rub her back, no don't rub her back. She never made up her mind in that room what she wanted so no wonder you went back into your head into your own thoughts. Yes, it happened – the song came back again.

Your Character by Association is Under Threat

In the most intense part of the birthing experience demands were given and these are out of the ordinary demands. One being asked to get her drugs; real drugs and she meant drugs. Basically, she had worked her way through the hospital pain relief entitlement and still wanted more. Where the hell do women think men can find drugs in a maternity unit? There are no vending machines that the local drug dealer stocks up just in case a woman wants more than her entitled prescribed pain relief. There was even a moment she started labelling names you had never heard of telling you once that your friends must know how to get hold of the stuff. No character references will be required from her thankfully as you have no idea who she thinks you associate yourself with.

Seriously, women just don't realise their demands and anyway since when would she condone this? Even when you tried to divert her back to the gas and air, she moaned. The requests inside that room simply become ludicrous. There was no way you were getting her any more drugs – one because you don't want to get into trouble and secondly, she was already high as a kite on gas and air. This is where it was your fault again and you will accept full responsibility for it.

Why Wasn't Recording Allowed?

There was a moment that you wanted to take your phone out and record what she was saying as it was so funny. The gas and air will create moments you would love to record and share out to your phone's contact list, as this is the opposite to how she behaves in front of others. You will laugh so much and want to capture each moment – but don't. It will not end well. Honestly you will be warned to stop the smirking and just don't even think about it and just put the phone away. And no, trying to record from different angles with the phone in your pocket won't work either.

That Song Always Returns

The moment the midwife said the baby's head was crowning, you started to hear the song louder than ever and tried your hardest to divert to the centre stage, with a front row seat to see the final push. The moment everyone was waiting for, the moment you got to meet your baby (and for some, the moment you passed out). The last few minutes were like waiting for the winning penalty to happen. You looked on to see the head appear and just as she went to score with the final push, it disappeared again. Your reactions were filled with anticipation and disappointment, all of which your partner was noticing and giving a look of, 'That is not helpful.' With the final push, the baby was here, and the fatherhood journey really did begin.

The Birth Story Lottery

The divide of men: those who wish they had cemented their feet into the ground so that they didn't faint, and those who stand centre stage in amazement at the size a vagina can be stretched to!

From the final push it will determine not only the next few moments of a man's life in 'The Road to Fatherhood' but a recorded response from everyone concerned on how he handled himself in that room. Despite all the hard work and support given, the final moments could wipe out any supportive story to one that will forever be told by your partner in a funny way.

The Cord Cutter

Front row seat, ready to cut the cord. Blood and all never bothered you and there was no way someone else was getting to that cord before you. You stepped up to the challenge and may never see your partner's vagina in the same light again after being at centre stage, but you stayed around to watch it being stitched as it just amazed you at their neat handiwork!

The Hand Holder

More back row than front row here, for this would have been you if you had dreaded looking down at centre stage as the thought of seeing a stretched vagina will forever scar your mind. You didn't want to chance fainting so played it safe in holding her hand during pushing. Known as the supportive partner by the Mum Squad and being a chicken by the Men Squad.

The Fainter

There was no seat involved, you hit the floor and stayed there. The whole experience got the better of you and whilst the baby was being pushed, you were being waved down with a fan to bring you around. You hoped no one noticed but they did and told everyone, in fact both the Mum Squad and the Men Squad united here in laughing afterwards.

Congratulations, It's Chaos!

Your cue to return back to work as it is not the planned leave you quite expected.

YOU WILL RECALL THAT most men are envious of the extended maternity leave that women get, however, the weeks following the birth are a time when men are glad to be at work. Yes, they want to be at home bonding with their baby, but they cannot handle the chaos! The whole house becomes a baby operation of keeping this baby fed, changed and trying to get them to sleep. It really isn't the maternity leave you both expected to happen.

The Divide of the Men Squad Members

There are two kinds of us men when it comes down to the first few months of chaos. The men who are hands on and men who are not. But the men who are hands on give other men a bad name, they get frowned upon. The Mum Squad love the hands-on dads, watching them balance the night feeds, the nappies, housework and receiving unlimited praise from the women around them. As for the other men, what some people don't understand is that us men don't always know what to do. We are suddenly given a little bundle at birth and then the shoulders back and chin up method doesn't work anymore – you search the internet for a manual on how to become a father overnight but fall asleep mid-search because fatherhood is exhausting.

Breastfeeding is Taking Away Our Boobs

They were our boobs first and now they are not. That's not fair – let's move on before the Mum Squad hear this. The Men Squad will not win this perspective.

Where are Our Gifts?

Visitors will swarm the house to visit the baby and bring gifts galore. Why is it though when visitors arrive, they bring something for the new baby and mummy but nothing for the daddy? Did we not experience the full nine months of rollercoaster emotions and twists and squeezed body parts during the birth?

You will notice the Mum Squad will always ask how the mother is doing, checking she is OK. The Men Squad however, will ask both the mother and father, how they are doing – thank you Men Squad for remembering we went through it too. At least they got a bed during the birth, all birthing partners get is an uncomfortable chair.

Supermarket Trips

Stay clear – they are chaos! Recommend home delivery service is there for a reason – the suggestion will get you brownie points and keep you out of the aisle chaos.

The Men Squad

Where not many words are needed, just a shared understanding that not one man really knows what he is doing but pretends to have it all under control regardless.

L IKE THE MUM SQUAD who support women, us men have the Men Squad who consist not only of fathers but single men too, who all know what is about to come next. Their sole job is telling the father-to-be that there is no way back and their life is over with now. Yes, even the happy celebratory dads are sought out to remind them that having a baby will change everything including their sex life, because babies are the contraceptive that they should have taken in the beginning, unless it was a planned moment. The father-to-be will receive sarcastic comments to reinforce that they have no idea what they are letting themselves in for. They become the target of jokes and sarcasm in every male crowd (obviously without the women present!).

Two beers later and the father-to-be will be comforted by the Men Squad, all feeling sorry for what the next eighteen years will bring. There will be the odd man who pops his head in to say, 'Actually it was the best moment of my life,' but he will be silenced with a packet of crisps and another beer because the Men Squad are all about preparing this man and father-to-be for entering the unknown territory of fatherhood.

Unlike the Mum Squad, the Men Squad try to keep their distance and only support if called upon, they know exactly what is in store and do not want to burden this man any more. It is simply a journey he will have to uncover himself, with a slight hint that everything from then on will be their fault – and they mean everything – even the two lines they have just had confirmed.

There concludes the first part of 'The Road to Fatherhood' and there is only one thing left for us men to say and that is – yes, those two little eyes can see everything for sure!

MESSAGE FROM

Jo x

THE ROAD TO MOTHERHOOD SERIES

Message from Jo

Firstly, thank you from the bottom of my heart for picking up the first book in 'The Road to Motherhood' series. I hope it's taken you back to the beginning of your own journey – whether that was a few months, years or decades ago – and given you a reason to smile, laugh, and maybe even shed a tear or two. My wish is that this book reminds you that you were doing a good job back then, even on the days when you felt like a total mess, because let's be honest, none of us ever really felt like we had it all together – and still don't!

Out of the 368,000 babies born every day across the world, there isn't a single woman who is truly prepared for what's to come. No manual, no rulebook – just pure chaos and an overwhelming love that somehow makes it all worthwhile. We're all just figuring it out as we go along, piecing together advice from others while trying to navigate our own version of motherhood.

Society loves to throw expectations at us – how we should feel, how we should look, how we should parent. The reality is, we don't fit into neat little boxes, and that's OK – and our children are so different from one to another. It's time to challenge those outdated norms and start embracing the messy, unpredictable, beautiful chaos that is motherhood. We've inherited so many expectations from generations before us – ideas of what a 'good mum' should look like, act like, and even feel like. But let's be honest – no one else is walking in your shoes, and no one else is juggling your reality.

Let's break free from the idea that there's a perfect way to do this. There isn't. You've got your own story, your own unique journey, and it's just as valid as anyone else's. Whether you became a mum at 22, 32, or 42 – whether it was planned or a total surprise, whether you were elated or terrified when you saw those two lines – you did it. You embraced the chaos and made it your own.

It doesn't matter how perfectly prepared you thought you were. Whether you were the woman with the colour-coded birth plan or the one winging it with a half-packed hospital bag, you made it through. Maybe you were the glowing mum-to-be, or maybe you were the one heaving at the smell of toast. However it happened, it was right for you and that's what matters.

One of the biggest lessons I've learned is that motherhood doesn't come with guarantees or blueprints. Sometimes it comes with piles of laundry, sleepless nights, and tantrums from both your kids and you at times! It's about survival some days, and pure magic on others.

And through it all, you just keep going – figuring it out one day at a time. Then there are these moments, whether it's looking at your children sleeping, seeing them achieve something or them telling you they love you – it's these little moments that remind you that becoming a mum is your biggest accomplishment by far, and the biggest lesson of how to love unconditionally.

And then there's your body – oh, how it changes! Motherhood shapes us in more ways than one, and sometimes we're our own harshest critics when it comes to our reflection in the mirror. Society tells us what we're supposed to look like, as if stretch marks and saggy bits somehow make us less beautiful, but the truth is, every line tells a story. Every change is a chapter of your journey to bring life into this world. Your body is powerful, resilient, and uniquely yours. Love it for all that it's done and continues to do.

For every new mum out there, or those who have been on the road to motherhood for years, it's easy to look back and feel guilty about what you could have done differently. Maybe you wished you'd spent more time cuddling your newborn or worried less about keeping the house spotless. But hindsight doesn't change the fact that you did the best you could with what you had at the time. You loved with all your heart, you protected them, and you grew as a woman – just like your little ones did.

It's funny how we look back on those early days and laugh at the things that felt so overwhelming at the time. The things we once cried about now make us smile because we've grown and learned from every single messy, beautiful moment. And now, as you turn the last few pages, I just want to say that you're doing an incredible job. Never let anyone tell you otherwise.

Own your story – every messy, chaotic, and winning part of it. 'The Road to Motherhood' is different for all of us, but the one thing we all have in common is that we're just trying our best to navigate it.

So, here's to you, to the road you've travelled, and to the one still ahead. Keep laughing, keep loving, and most of all, keep being unapologetically you. Motherhood doesn't change who you are – it just adds another layer to your story. Be proud of every single bit of it.

And remember, there's no perfect way to be a mum – there's just your way. Embrace it, own it, and know that you're never alone on this journey. Thank you for walking with me on 'The Road to Motherhood.' Until the next book – keep being the incredible woman and mum that you are.

With lots of love and laughter,

Jo x

FOUNDER OF:

The Road to Motherhood Book Series

Connect With Jo

The Limitless Legacy Movement

www.connectwithjo.com

THE REAL MOTHERHOOD

Diaries

A special thank you to the women featured in The Real Motherhood Diaries who have shared their stories of once seeing their own two lines

With Thanks To:

Kayla Middleton

Samantha-Jane Littlejohns

Jean Bigg

Nat Baines

Laura Guy

Lisa Williams

Janine Friston

Nic Gray

Amanda Alcock

Samantha Slater

Emily Grey

Hannah Barker

Katie Cheeseman

Lauren Robinson

Anerleigh Roots-Taylor

The Real Motherhood Diaries

'Behind every motherhood journey is a woman trying to navigate the biggest change in her life, both physically and emotionally. It is only when we read real life stories, we feel heard, united and never alone again.' – Joanne Cook

Joanne's Story of Discovering Two Lines:

'DISCOVERING YOU ARE PREGNANT inside a supermarket toilet on your way to work was not the ideal dream location of discovering the famous two lines, but when you have a voice in your head that says, 'You are pregnant,' numerous times on your way to work, there is no other option but to get it confirmed! I was about to hand in my notice for a job to give me a big step up in the corporate ladder and had a big white wedding planned for the following year. Yes, 'Oh crap!' does not begin to summarise my response in seeing those two lines! But looking back now, they were the best sign I could ever receive. Not only were they an introduction to the boy who got to call me mum but the sign that my life was going to change forever in the best way possible. Even the shocked moments turn out to be the best moments of my life (not at the time though, as I had no idea how I was going to fit into my wedding dress!). You will however be glad to know that receiving my two lines with my second son was in fact in the comfort of my own toilet as it was a less of a shock factor.'

Joanne Cook – Mum to two sons, Jack and Billy

Author of The Road to Motherhood Book Series and Founder of www.connectwithjo.com

Kayla's Story of Discovering Two Lines:

'I'd always envisioned telling my husband in a really romantic way, however the reality actually consisted of me having a panic attack in our honeymoon villa! I walked out of the bathroom in a panicked sob, threw the test at him and ran back in to vomit. Leaving him on the bed bewildered and quite confused! In my defence, we had just come back from an 'all you can drink' sunset cruise so alcohol certainly played a part in my vomiting freakout!'

Kayla Middleton – Mum to one son, Jayden

https://lp.affirmation-army.co.uk/elevate-the-membership

Samantha's Story of Discovering Two Lines:

'I remember the moment like it was yesterday – after years of being told it would be nearly impossible to conceive, seeing those two little lines felt surreal. Shock, fear, and an overwhelming wave of joy all collided in that instant, and I dared to dream of glowing through pregnancy like the women in magazines. But reality had other plans. My days were filled with constant nausea, unpredictable mood swings, and aches that left me feeling anything but radiant. While my friends seemed to glide through pregnancy effortlessly, I was riddled with guilt for struggling to enjoy it, often feeling like I was failing before I'd even begun.

'Then, everything changed when my baby arrived 9.5 weeks early. The fear was overwhelming as he was whisked away to the neonatal ward and not being able to see him for 24 hours, or hold him for nearly a week, was a heartbreak I couldn't put into words. The guilt of my earlier struggles now seemed trivial compared to the helplessness of watching my tiny baby fight for every breath. It was a whirlwind of emotions – fear, guilt, exhaustion – but the moment I finally held him in my arms, his tiny hand gripping mine, every tear, every doubt, and every struggle felt worth it. In that moment, I knew we were both stronger than I'd ever imagined.'

Samantha-Jane Littlejohns – Mum to two sons, Connor and Declan

www.thehabitsofhappiness.co.uk

Jean's Story of Discovering Two Lines:

'I had been trying for ages but couldn't fall pregnant and was under the doctor to try to work out why, but they just didn't know why it wasn't happening. Then suddenly it just happened. I was pregnant! I was so happy when the doctor did a test and told me I was going to be a mum. Now I am a mother of two daughters, a grandmother of five granddaughters and grandmother to their partners who I love as my own grandsons. I also have thirteen great-grandchildren. I love them all and enjoy spending time together. I have so many fond memories, especially the days we would all meet on Fridays, and I would buy the turkey legs for the rolls at lunchtime. I don't just have two daughters; I have a big family. I love them all so much.'

Jean Bigg, nee Blanchard, queen of the family to four generations – Mum to two daughters, Lorraine and Jackie

Nat's Story of Discovering Two Lines:

'When I found out I was pregnant I was shocked – it happened fairly quickly, a fact that is not lost on me when so many cannot conceive easily. Previous miscarriages (many years earlier) meant I couldn't help but feel apprehensive and worried. I also thought I'd have more time to get healthier and wiser (still working on that one). But amidst it all, there was an overwhelming sense of joy, that something that I had longed for, for so long – might now be in reach.'

Nat Baines – Mum to one son, Oscar

www.TheProfessionalPlanner.com

Laura's Story of Discovering Two Lines:

'As soon as I saw those two lines on the pregnancy test, I was overwhelmed with emotion – excited yet apprehensive about what was to come. Now, when I look at my kids, I see how much they've guided my personal growth and taught me about the depth of unconditional love. Through motherhood, I've discovered a strength and resilience I never knew I had. They've shown me the fierceness of a mother's love and the beauty of evolving alongside them.'

Laura Guy – Mum to two children, Alexia and Lucas

www.lauraguy.co.uk

Lisa's Story of Discovering Two Lines:

'Pregnancy wasn't an easy ride, after several miscarriages combined with a lockdown pregnancy and gestational diabetes. I had my challenges cut out for the whole nine months, gripped with fear of loss and lockdown. Whilst pregnant we had already chosen our daughter's name, we chose Talia which means rain, teamed up with Beau. Bringing them together as Talia-Beau meaning RAINBOW. Rainbow baby is the term used after a pregnancy loss. Holding my real-life Rainbow in my arms was greater than any pot of gold I could find, that feeling holding her in my arms was the most incredible feeling.'

Lisa Williams – Mum to two girls, Alysa and Talia-Beau

www.lisawilliams-lmg.co.uk

Janine's Story of Discovering Two Lines:

'"This can't be real!" This was my initial thought when I took my pregnancy test. I'm not ready, not sure I'll ever be ready to be a Mum. I don't even like children that much, all that mess and having to speak excitedly childish to little people – that's not me! And I definitely can't play with dolls or dress-up! But something changed when it was my children. I loved seeing them have fun, learn new skills and share Mum and son play time. Seeing them grow into little people with their own personalities, and now as they develop into young adults – it's amazing.'

Janine Friston – Mum to two teenage boys

www.femalebusinessnetwork.co.uk

Nic's Story of Discovering Two Lines:

'I found out I had PCOS after trying for a baby for nearly 8 months. As I was a bit older, I decided we should go down the route of checking all was OK. After booking in the first lot of tests I found out I was pregnant! From thinking we might not be able to conceive to seeing those lines, it was such an amazing feeling!'

Nic Gray – Mum of two

www.facebook.com/nicgray.co.uk

Amanda's Story of Discovering Two Lines:

'I put off taking the test for a few days, although I knew in my heart I was pregnant because I felt different. When I saw the lines, I was nervous and excited, it confirmed it was real. I look back now and struggle to remember life before Emily and wouldn't change it for the world.'

Amanda Alcock – Mum to one daughter, Emily

www.randompanda.co.uk

Samantha's Story of Discovering Two Lines:

'It was a dismal January day, and I sat in a meeting room with senior management planning out the year... my boss turned to me and said I'm not accepting any resignations, I need you to be here to see this through. I smiled and wondered. I was late. I'd been late before and the test was negative, but this time, it was actually positive. I calculated maternity leave would start in September... I tried not to daydream, I'd been disappointed too many times, but oh my gosh, I'd love to be in my perfect house, cooking healthy meals, whilst the kids played happily (now I know that is a myth!!). I snapped back to reality as everyone started leaving the room. Myles, my husband, had flown off to Boston that morning so I went home to our dogs and as I cooked my dinner, thought about whether I should have a glass of wine. I remember looking at my dogs and wondering how they would be with kids. Then it all got too much, I knew I should wait, but I had to know. I ran upstairs and grabbed a test. I know everyone says it feels like forever waiting for those lines, or in my case pregnant or not pregnant (I'm the sort of girl that needs absolute) but that wasn't what felt like hours... It was waiting for my husband to ring. When I took the test, he was still 30,000 feet in the air, and it felt like forever. FINALLY, five hours later my phone rang, and I couldn't wait to hear what he had to say, I shouted, "It's POSITIVE!" I started dreaming of leaving behind my stressful job that I would have enjoyed if I didn't have to work with some of the people, for a year of being a mother. Little did I know that my idea of being a Stepford wife/mother, was so far from the truth... the birth was traumatic, not to mention the reconstructive surgery needed! But I didn't learn my lesson, because I did it a second time (although I was clued up that time!)... and I could not love two humans any more than I love my kids. They frustrate and amaze in equal measures! But they are incredible!'

Samantha Slater – Mum to two, Tilly and Sebby

www.SamanthaJaneSlater.com

Emily's Story of Discovering Two Lines:

'It was a few days after my 18th birthday celebrations that I realised I was pregnant, which raised immediate feelings of mum guilt! Little did I know then that mum's guilt never goes away! I wouldn't change a thing, and I'm proud I stuck to my desire to bring into the world a bundle of pleasure to love and nurture, against everyone else's advice!'

Emily Grey – Mum of four, Ayden, Erin, Safia and Samuel

www.Emswellbeing.co.uk

Hannah's Story of Discovering Two Lines:

'I was so excited to see those two lines on my pregnancy test, but also very anxious and scared after suffering miscarriages. I finally had hope that filled me with so much joy! Throughout my pregnancy journey I did struggle to believe all was well because I suffered a miscarriage six months prior to becoming pregnant again, six months later, with my now eight-year-old – who brings me so much joy! Our journey together wasn't the easiest of rides, she suffered a lot with really bad reflux which was really difficult as she would spend hours screaming in pain with an undiagnosed cow's milk allergy. I took her back to the doctors three times until on the last appointment they found the reason for all the screaming was to do with the cow's milk allergy she had! Once we found the right milk which worked for her, she was like a different baby and she began to thrive. In all her development milestones, I did have a lot of new mum friends whose babies were doing a lot of things before Peyton did. Being a first-time mum, I did struggle, especially because Peyton was quite a late walker and crawler compared to my friends' babies, but what I came to realise was children develop at different rates and there's not a one size fits all. Having been trained as a childcare expert with my nursery nurse background and recently teaching assistant background, I did find that I put a lot of pressure on the milestones as to why she was so behind when in reality she just did everything in her own time frame. Fast forward to having my other children I released the pressure and went with the flow, so I didn't have the high expectations, I just allowed them to all develop at their own rate. I did suffer from postnatal depression and struggled to bond with my daughter initially but now we have such a strong bond, and we are like best friends, I love her so much. She is so special with her being my rainbow baby.'

Hannah Barker – Mum of four, Peyton, Maciee, Evan, Rafe

https://www.facebook.com/GratitudeMummentor

Katie's Story of Discovering Two Lines:

'The wait felt like hours, waiting with anticipation for the two lines to appear. Then there they were! Two lines to confirm that I was pregnant. A sense of nerves as it was real and happening. I had this burst of joy and excitement that my journey as a mummy was about to start, something I had always wanted.'

Katie Cheeseman – Mum of three, Ryan, Charlie and Ronnie

Lauren's Story of Discovering Two Lines:

'My first pregnancy with Robyn was a complete shock! I instinctively knew the test was positive before I looked at it and the same was true for my son years later. With my first pregnancy I felt no fear or worry around being a mum, perhaps because I was 24, however, with my son after longing for another child for so long I instantly felt scared and worried due to health complications in my first pregnancy. The weight of telling others felt heavy and I was very aware of the risks. I found out I was pregnant during lockdown and immediately felt the impact of that, feeling lonely and isolated and struggling with PTSD. Looking back, having my daughter unplanned and so quickly with a new partner changed my life for the better. Without her I wouldn't be the person I am today, and it feels like I knew this immediately. I wouldn't change my son for the world, but the pregnancy in my mental state during lockdown was a very tough time.'

Lauren Robinson – Mum of two, Robyn and Andrew

Anerleigh's Story of Discovering Two Lines:

'The minute I found out I literally screamed, 'What the f*ck!' I couldn't quite believe it! I had fertility struggles and was considering IVF so falling naturally was not an option in my mind! I did another five tests to make sure I wasn't seeing things!

Seeing her now fills me with joy, but what a rollercoaster it has been!'

Anerleigh Roots-Taylor – Mum to one daughter, Wynter

www.leighsianmusic.co.uk

About the Author

Joanne Cook is the founder of Connect With Jo and the creator of The Road to Motherhood book series. As an intuitive life and business mentor, she creates spaces where women feel seen, stand out with confidence, and lead impactful businesses that drive the change they want to see in the world.

A mum of two with over 23 years on the motherhood journey herself, Joanne understands the reality of balancing personal growth, career dreams, and raising a family. In July 2002, she became a mum for the first time at the age of twenty-two. Ambitious and driven, she quickly realised the unspoken pressures women face when trying to "do it all" – especially when navigating a career alongside motherhood.

Joanne's journey took her from the corporate world into the education sector. But by 2018, she found herself facing her third burnout – a result of running life and business on autopilot while juggling the endless demands of mum life. Guided by intuition and purpose, she made the courageous decision to walk away from the successful business she had built, later leaving the financial security of full-time employment to launch Connect With Jo – her soul-led business supporting women to lead with purpose, freedom, and authenticity.

Joanne created The Road to Motherhood book series to shine a light on the parts of motherhood often left out of the highlight reel – the messy, emotional, laugh-out-loud, and quietly powerful moments that shape us as women. This series isn't just about babies and birth plans; it's about identity, resilience, choices, and the generational journey – from those first two lines to watching your children grow into adults of their own.

Her mission goes beyond storytelling. Joanne supports the next generation of female leaders – women building impactful businesses, raising families, and choosing to leave legacies that stretch far beyond income. Her work empowers women to reclaim their voice, own their story, and lead lives aligned with who they truly are – not just what the world expects them to be. Joanne has recently launched The Working Mums Network – a high-level, one-of-a-kind space designed for women who are serious about building impactful businesses. This isn't just another network; it's a powerful space for connection, collaboration, and confidence – where ambitious women come together to grow, support, and succeed on their own terms whilst helping each other to rise.

She is deeply passionate about helping women create more freedom in their lives and businesses, allowing them to reach their goals with confidence and ease. Joanne believes that every woman holds the power to shape her destiny and live a life of purpose and fulfilment. And when you're in Joanne's world, something shifts – you begin to believe in yourself like never before.

To find out more about working with Jo or joining her free community – where she helps you master your mindset, align your energy, and build strategic foundations to grow an impactful business, step into your role as a legacy leader, and create a legacy beyond income, visit:

www.connectwithjo.com

To Explore The Road to Motherhood Series and Upcoming Events:

www.theroadtomotherhood.com

For further information on Working Mums Network, a high-level, one-of-a-kind space designed for ambitious women who are serious about building impactful businesses, visit:

www.workingmumsnetwork.com

The next journey on The Road to Motherhood will be out soon

Don't miss out on all The Road to Motherhood book series updates and to be the first to hear about the release of book number two, which will be released soon – you will not want to miss it!

Printed in Dunstable, United Kingdom